With Lifespan Integration, Peggy Pace has discovered a revolutionary psychotherapy for trauma, dissociation and attachment disorders. Her book is comprehensive and gives the reader a thorough description of the neu-roscience underlying LI, and an excellent overview of the LI protocols and treatment options. Peggy Pace's writing is clear, bright and stimulating. A "must read" for anyone interested in LI.

Joanna Smith, Psychologist - Paris, France
Co-author of Trauma and Resilience.

After more than 25 years as a practicing psychotherapist, I discovered Lifespan Integration. LI has taken me far above my expectations. As I began using LI with my clients, I and they saw huge improvements in their healing processes. In my ongoing quest to go deeper into myself, I experienced LI as a client, and found that with LI I could go even deeper into my inner exploration than had been possible with previous therapies. A whole new positive energy comes from this work. There is no magic, though. If the client has had deep traumas, LI therapy can be painful at times; however the potential for deep healing is there.

Here is how I explain what happens: When we are born, we come to life with a lens that allows us to perceive the world. That lens, if kept clean and protected from scratches by nurturing and protective caregivers, will allow an individual to accurately see his or her world. If the infant or young child has been neglected or mistreated during early development, the lens accumulates dust and moisture or scratches which create blind spots. These blind spots limit the perception of the person during his or her entire life. As a therapist, I could recognize those blind spots within myself and within my clients, but never was able to make a satisfying correction. I have found Lifespan Integration to be an excellent tool for healing and 'cleaning' the lens. Once the lens is cleaned or corrected, a better connection with the soul is established, and the Light with all its healing benefits comes through, restoring intelligence, creativity, imagination, etc. Aristotle says: "The entelechy of the acorn is to be a tree". I can affirm that LI has put me in touch with my own entelechy.

Dr Ronald H Riopel, Psychologist - Montréal, Québec, Canada

Growing up during the Soviet regime in Russia, under an atmosphere of suffering and violence, my nervous system was primed only for survival. For most of my life my intimate relationships only repeated the patterns of my childhood, bringing new pain and despair. Eighteen years of undergoing various forms of therapy, trying to find a way to heal the traumas of my childhood, led me only to the realization of my own helplessness and my inability to change these patterns.

Lifespan Integration therapy was, for me, the door to a new life. Using this incredible tool which she developed, Peggy released me from a lifetime of pain and fear, replacing these early legacies instead with love, support and security. With LI my body-mind was reformed naturally in a new way. Through LI I became the person I was meant to be - free and happy.

Yulia Zhirova, Psychologist - St.Petersburg, Russia; and Narva, Estonia

---

From the very beginning of my practice in psychology, I have always searched for a way of healing people completely, not just helping them to cope with their suffering, but repairing the very foundations of their psychic structure. I found Lifespan Integration to be the answer, both for my personal healing and my professional results. Moreover, Peggy Pace has such a simple, clear and concise manner to help us understand this revolutionary method...her book is very accessible. However, be careful not to confuse simplicity of words to indicate lack of substance; because LI is a method whose depth and complexity can only be truly understood through experience. So, go ahead, read about it, but know that reading this book is only a start if you really want to be in connection with yourself and with others.

Élise Castonguay, Psychologist - Quebec, Canada.

By creating Lifespan Integration Peggy Pace has offered the world an innovative, brilliant, elegant and efficient approach to healing and integrating a wide range of trauma and thus restoring the person's integrity of body-mind and his/her emotional well-being. LI permits also to heal early attachment issues, and to shift from neglect of oneself to a healthy self esteem, self compassion and the expression of our authentic self. Relying on the power of attunement between therapist and client, it establishes at the same time clear boundaries in the inter- and intrapersonal space.

Being originally a trained molecular biologist, I particularly appreciate the coherence of LI with the known neurobiological processes. LI is actually the psychotherapy I use daily and it is much appreciated by my clients.

Thank you, Peggy!"

Dr. Anandi Janner Steffan, Neuchâtel, Suisse

LIFESPAN INTEGRATION
Connecting Ego States *Through* Time

Peggy Pace

EIRENE IMPRINT

To
Aaron and Roslyn
who taught me how to converse with children
and most of what I know about child development

In memory of my father
William Roby Pace Jr. MD
who encouraged me to think for myself,
and instilled in me his enthusiasm for learning

Book Design by Marrowstone Design, www.marrowstonedesign.com
Cover and back photographs by Galen Garwood, © 2015

ISBN: 978-0-9760603-6-9
Printed in the United States of America
Information about how to purchase this book is available at the Lifespan Integration website: http://LifespanIntegration.com

"A human being is a part of the whole, called by us 'Universe', a part limited in time and space. He experiences himself, his thoughts and feelings, as something separated from the rest...a kind of optical delusion of his consciousness. This delusion is a kind of prison for us, restricting us to our personal desires and to affection for a few persons nearest to us. Our task must be to free ourselves from this prison by widening our circle of compassion to embrace all living creatures and the whole of nature in its beauty."

Albert Einstein

CONTENTS

ACKNOWLEDGEMENTS

Special thanks go to my clients without whom I could never have developed Lifespan Integration. Their ongoing willingness to allow me to try new ideas and new methods in their therapy, and to answer my myriad questions about what worked and what didn't work, has guided me over the years to the method (outlined in this book) which I use today.

I want to acknowledge the multitudes of teachers, healers, energy workers, and seers who work tirelessly and synergistically from many angles to heal our planet and its inhabitants. In particular I want to thank my personal friends and energy workers, Darlene Gray and Charlene Christian. When, unbeknownst to Dar and Char, I began using Lifespan Integration to treat some of the clients we shared, these wise sisters "saw" the energetic changes LI was producing in our mutual clients. Their enthusiasm about the new work I was doing was a welcomed affirmation during the early stages of LI's development.

Heartfelt gratitude goes to my friend and colleague, Catherine Thorpe, who has been extraordinarily helpful throughout my process of going public with Lifespan Integration. Catherine was the first therapist I trained in my new method, and her shared enthusiasm helped me realize the importance of writing this book and of making the Lifespan Integration method of therapy available to other therapists around the world. Catherine provided LI with the fitting name: *Lifespan Integration,* and, most importantly, she skillfully practiced the Lifespan Integration protocol with me as her subject, allowing me to experience first hand the therapy I was developing, as I was developing it.

I would like to also express my thanks to Michael Berni for teaching me about systems, and to Richard Christy for sharing with me his insights and his expertise in EMDR.

I feel greatly indebted to all the computer whizzes past and present who spend their days making my life easier and making the world more accessible to me. I can only imagine how much more difficult it would have been for me had I attempted to write this book with a pen or typewriter, and without the resources of the world wide web. I feel very fortunate to live in an age where one can magically cut and paste, format, create bullets, or delete, simply by clicking the mouse. Also thanks to computer science, and to the advent of the internet, no matter how far from "civilization" I choose to live, I am able to order any book I need, and research almost any subject, right from my laptop.

Many thanks to all the computer genii.

FOREWORD

My friend and colleague, Peggy Pace and I travelled together to a psychotherapy workshop being held in the beautiful San Juan Islands of British Columbia, Canada. The evening before we traveled to the workshop, Peggy asked me if I would like to experience a new method of therapy which she had personally developed. When I agreed, she asked me to recall an experience from my life that I wanted to heal. I focused on a painful memory scene from my adolescence, re-activating the emotions, images and bodily sensations from that difficult earlier experience. Peggy then led me through a chronological timeline of actual memories from my life, starting right after the difficult memory and ending in the present moment. We repeated this several times. Within an hour or so, the fears, heartache, and body sensations associated with the traumatic experience were gone. The next morning I awakened with a new clarity and freedom about the trauma that I had never before experienced, and the healing has remained.

After the two day workshop, as we traveled back to Seattle through Puget Sound on the ferry boat, Peggy and I discussed the new method she had developed. Peggy told me that she had been using this same method with her clients, and they were also noting significant changes after multiple repetitions of their timelines. As our discussion continued, Peggy asked, "What shall we call this therapy?"

I offered, "Lifespan Integration."

Peggy responded, "I agree. I think we should call it Lifespan Integration — LI for short."

We looked out the ferry windows and saw a group of Pacific white-sided dolphins leaping through the air along both sides of the boat. Something tremendous had begun.

Today Lifespan Integration is being taught in many countries around the world. Knowledge of LI has spread rapidly as newly trained therapists tell their colleagues about their successes using LI to treat trauma, emotional issues, relational problems, dissociative disorders and many other typical concerns which clients bring to therapy. Lifespan Integration therapists around the world find that people change on deep and profound levels after they have experienced Peggy Pace's new method of therapy.

With LI, we consistently find that patients are relieved of their distresses without being re-traumatized, even though we are targeting very painful memories. The titration between recalling a difficult scene and timeline repetitions relieves clients' distress without over-activating them. Additionally, no secondary traumatization occurs for the therapist when Lifespan Integration is used for counseling. I personally have heard hundreds of very difficult stories, but I carry only gratitude and awe from the change that takes place in front of me within an hour or so of LI.

One of my favorite outcomes with Lifespan Integration is the innate, organic information that becomes available within clients as we move them through the LI process. Invariably, as a clinician takes a client through the steps of LI, not only does the client's distress decrease, but they become aware of positive, truthful information within them. Two examples of this emerging awareness from my clinical practice are, "Now I understand my mother actually loved me, but she was not equipped to take care of a new baby as an 18-year-old girl," and, "Something that I always thought was my fault was not my fault at all! Circumstances out of my control caused the bad thing to happen." Clinicians have worked very hard over the years to instill these types of beliefs into clients. We find they spontaneously emerge with LI.

Therapies are available today which appear to change clients on a mind-body level. Lifespan Integration is such a therapy. With it, we have the opportunity to help patients do more than talk about their problems. People who go to counseling are often frustrated that something they have talked about many times, and often over many years, has not changed to the degree that clients need. In the many years I have been using LI, I have not had a client return and ask to target the same issue in the same way again. Lifespan Integration is a method that appears to work on a deeper level than talk therapy alone. As the two examples above portray, we see clients change ineffective ways of thinking when they are guided through the timeline process. This is one of the benefits of Lifespan Integration.

Peggy has created, developed and refined Lifespan Integration over many years. The work she puts forward in this text is a compilation of her scientific background, her understanding of neuroscience and interpersonal neurobiology, and her innovation. We observe that Lifespan Integration appears to increase coherence and improve clients' overall ability to engage with life and relationships.

Thank you, Peggy.

Cathy Thorpe,
April 2015,
Author of *The Success and Strategies of Lifespan Integration*

INTRODUCTION

The human mind develops interactively in response to the environment of early childhood. Defensive systems that are created in response to a hostile early environment continue to operate in the present, mostly out of consciousness, even when they are no longer needed. In early stages of human development, the self is not unified, but rather many selves and self-states are developed to respond to varying conditions and circumstances. During the process of normal development these selves and self-states are integrated. How integration occurs is still being researched, but it is believed that multiple selves are connected across time and across contexts through the co-construction of autobiographical life narratives between parent and child.

When children grow up in an environment of trauma or neglect, or both, they develop many different selves and self-states. When parental support is lacking, or when children are prohibited from discussing the traumatic events they experience, or both, the co-construction of narratives required for neural integration does not occur. For these individuals, many selves and self-states are only partially integrated and end up being held in the neural system separately. Dissociative identity disorder results when children experience overwhelming trauma in the absence of support and protection from adult caretakers. In these cases there is insufficient neural integration for the creation of a unified self.

Dissociation exists on a continuum throughout the population. There are many individuals who do not experience or feel a coherent sense of self across time, and to them this feels normal. Clients who have little or no memory of their childhoods often fall into this category. Through my work developing and using Lifespan Integration with clients, I have become more aware of how pervasive dissociation is throughout the population. Through repeated use of Lifespan Integration people become more and more integrated, and report feeling more solid inside, more adult, more capable and competent.

Our neurological systems are designed to alert us to and protect us from perceived dangers. The defensive systems we create in childhood stay with us, needed or not. During Lifespan Integration, repeated journeys through the Time Line of memories and images enable the client's neural system to bypass outmoded defensive neurological networks while creating new networks which are more useful and adaptive. What a five-year-old perceives as a danger would most likely not present a problem to a forty-year-old, and yet the defensive structure designed by the five-year-old nervous system remains encoded, and comes into play more frequently than that forty-year-old may realize. Lifespan Integration is extremely efficient in its ability to track directly to the archaic defensive strategy, insert new and current information, and connect the associated ego state (neural network) to the current operating system, the adult self of the client. The client is then led through the Time Line of memories and images which integrates the ego state (neural network) to the whole self system. Clients often want to avoid certain time periods and memories because of the associated emotional, and sometimes physical pain. It is important to explain to the client how going through the Time Line of images "connects the dots" to eventually create the whole picture of the integrated self.

I have found that unresolved grief and the inability to let go of the past and move forward is at the heart of much of the distress which I see in clients in their present lives. Often the integration of the split off child part can't take place until the individual is ready or able to let go of something from the past. When using the Lifespan Integration method to move forward from the past memory, any resistance toward moving forward will be immediately evident. The adult self of the client is connected to and dialoguing with the child ego state throughout the process, and can usually elicit from the child, through their internal dialogue, what it is that is keeping the child stuck in the past. The child ego state may feel she needs to remain in the past scene to care for siblings or a parent. Or perhaps the child from the past is still striving to get something from the parent such as love, approval, or attention. Sometimes it is necessary to bring imaginary resources into the past scene before the child self is ready to let go and move forward.

It is important to make it clear that "staying in the past" is not a real option for ego states or part-selves if healing is to take place. If an ego state chooses to remain in the past, that part of the self system will remain frozen in time and will not be integrated into the whole self-system. Parts that are not integrated remain outside of the control of the Self. They will act independently and will often act out in ways that are not helpful or useful to the whole self system. In many instances the acting out can be self-destructive. Once this is thoroughly understood, clients are usually willing to continue to dialogue and negotiate with their child ego states who are stuck in past time frames and resistant to moving forward in time.

When a child ego state resists integration, I instruct the adult client to tell her inner child that the past reality exists only as a memory, and that now the child lives in the present with the adult. I then have the adult client go through the Time Line of memories and images from the age of the stuck child part all the way to the present. The child ego state and the adult client use the same brain and visual cortex, and therefore the child self will also "see" the chronological memories and images which the adult client brings up, whether or not she feels willing to cooperate. After returning to the present via the Time Line, I instruct the adult client to re-enter the memory scene and to recommence the internal dialogue with the child ego state. Having seen the passage of time as portrayed by the images, the child part will now be partially integrated and may be more willing to cooperate. If the child ego state continues to be resistant to the process, I simply repeat the Time Line as many times as necessary. New memories and images or expanded aspects of the memories will spontaneously surface on each subsequent repetition. After sufficient repetitions of the Time Line of images, usually three to five repetitions, the child part will become fully integrated into the whole self system.

For many years as a therapist I've struggled with the question: "What is it that makes it so difficult for most humans to let go?" Cognitive therapy can give us understanding and tools for changing dysfunctional patterns, yet certain familiar conditions or circumstances will cause us to revert to more primitive feeling states and behaviors, even when we know better. Jungian therapeutic techniques such as dream work and active imagination bring progress on the emotional level, but these types of therapy are long term and are not affordable for most clients. Through reprocessing past traumas with EMDR, many people are able to truly let go of "old stuff" or "baggage" from their past. However EMDR doesn't work for everyone. We are cautioned against using EMDR with clients who dissociate, and when we do use EMDR with dissociative individuals we risk a dissociative reaction to the emotional material activated by the processing. When working with clients who are even more dissociative, the client may "switch" during EMDR processing, presenting separate ego states in such a way that any one state is not present long enough to complete the work he or she begins. EMDR processing can also be interrupted when clients with low affect tolerance become overwhelmed with emotion and "flood." When this happens EMDR processing remains incomplete, and there is a need for containment of the emotion that was activated by the EMDR processing.

Many clients who were traumatized or neglected as children have limited memories of their childhoods. These clients tend to be dissociative. They are often chronically anxious or depressed, and can be triggered by implicit bodily or sensory memories. Other clients who do have memories of their childhood traumas are easily flooded emotionally when triggered. Many clients who were traumatized as children have developed elaborate mechanisms which help them to avoid being emotionally triggered, but these same mechanisms often interfere significantly with their ability to lead a normal life. Lifespan Integration was originally developed to help adults who were traumatized or neglected when they were children, however LI has been found to be very effective with clients of all ages.

When using the Lifespan Integration method, time can be viewed as fluid in both directions. The current self can travel back in time to visit parts of the self who are arrested or frozen in the past. Likewise, the selves from the past can be brought forward in time, and can be integrated into the self system. Current information and security provided by a nurturing parental part of self can be taken back through time to help a part of the self who lacked these resources in the past. Younger ego states who have been isolated in a past time frame often have qualities to offer which can be of benefit to the self in the present. As neural integration proceeds through use of Lifespan Integration therapy, resources from both past and present become more and more available to the whole self system.

Prior to the twentieth century, families and communities were relatively stable. Before trains, cars, and airplanes entered our lives, human beings lived close to their extended families throughout their lifespans. With only horses and sailing vessels for transportation, only the most adventurous individuals would pack up and move across the state or country and away from parents, siblings, grandparents, uncles, aunts, cousins, and friends. Trauma, loss, and neglect have made unfortunate intrusions into children's lives throughout history, however until recently most children have had the benefit of living within an extended family system or tribe. Within these extended family environments, children have historically had many adults available who knew them and who could help them to make sense of their experiences.

Growing up within extended family systems provided children with the continuity of time and place needed for co-constructing their auto-biographical narratives. Cultural anthropology shows us that recounting stories about the tribe and about individuals within the tribe has been important cross-culturally and throughout history. For previous genera-tions, the co-construction of life narratives was an integral part of family and tribal life. In modern times, due to very recent cultural and sociolog-ical changes, children very often are raised in environments that lack the continuity of time and place. The lack of continuity in our lives today is reflected in the psychological problems that we see in our clients, friends, families, and selves. Lifespan Integration, through the mechanism of the Time Line of memories and images, offers a method of restoring some of what is missing.

The following chapters describe in more detail how Lifespan Integration can be used to heal past traumas and to bring about a more coherent and better functioning self-system in the present. Lifespan Integration is a rev-olutionary new method which heals by restructuring and integrating neural systems in the body-mind. In order to restructure, the client's system must disorganize and then reorganize. A therapist who attempts this method without proper training runs the risk of dysregulating a fragile client's self-system. Best outcomes with LI result when the therapist is coherent and energetically and emotionally present. Therapists who have done their own body-mind healing work will be better able to stay present with the client to contain the emotional material which comes up during LI processing. Therapists, psychologists, and psychiatrists who wish to use this new method are advised to attend a Lifespan Integration training workshop. At a training workshop, mental health practitioners observe Lifespan Integration sessions live and on DVD, and practice and experi-ence Lifespan Integration under supervision. For dates and locations of future trainings, see: *https://LifespanIntegration.com*.

Chapter One
Functions of Lifespan Integration

Lifespan Integration, as its name implies, is a new therapy that integrates neural structures and firing patterns throughout the body-mind, and across the lifespan. Lifespan Integration can be used to clear trauma or to build self structure or both, depending on the history and needs of the client. Repetitions of a visual and sensory timeline are unique to all the Lifespan Integration protocols.

The most dramatic application of Lifespan Integration therapy can be seen in the clearing of past or recent traumas using the LI PTSD protocol. Even the most entrenched cases of PTSD will resolve after one or two sessions of LI. An individual who was functional and able to operate in the world prior to a traumatic event will be able to return to his normal functioning immediately after one or two sessions of LI focused on the traumatic event. Any PTSD symptoms, including nightmares, intrusions, and flashbacks related to this traumatic event, will cease. The results are stable. Quality of life continues to improve over time after the traumatic event is cleared with Lifespan Integration.

Lifespan Integration can also be used to help clients overcome the effects of early trauma and neglect. Individuals whose early needs were not met, and those whose early environments were chaotic, inconsistent, or hostile will need many more sessions of Lifespan Integration therapy than will clients who are securely attached and who functioned well prior to a traumatic incident. Individuals who experienced early trauma or neglect will benefit most from the LI protocols which build self structure, change attachment patterns, and improve regulation of emotion.

Secure attachment in humans is engendered, beginning at birth, through an interactive process between parent and child. A securely attached parent is able to meet the early attachment needs of her newborn infant. An infant who is loved and cared for will understand at a deep level that he is important, lovable and valuable. He will grow up to be a securely attached adult. Human babies are born in a very vulnerable, unfinished state, with largely undeveloped nervous systems. Newborn babies are 'designed' to be in constant contact

1

with their mothers. Parents who had their own early needs met are usually capable of providing their infants with the physical and emotional environments conducive to optimal growth and development. A securely attached mother is able to remain attuned to her infant. This attunement allows the forming nervous system of the infant to sufficiently 'download' and internalize the needed neural structures for affect regulation and self-love. This interactive process continues for the first few years of the child's life, as his nervous system develops.

Emotion regulation is 'learned' within the parent-infant dyad. The attuned mother holds her infant within a tolerable range of emotions. Eventually the developing child internalizes this ability. Parents who are unable to regulate their own emotions are not able to attune to and regulate the emotions of their babies. Likewise, parents who are insecurely attached will unintentionally pass their insecure attachment styles on to their children. Even a very responsible and well intentioned parent, if insecurely attached, will lack the coherence needed to bring about a solid and secure self structure in his or her child. In addition, when infants and small children experience early trauma or neglect without the support of attuned and protective caretakers, they are unable to integrate segments of their experience. Without a coherent autobiographical narrative, these individuals will grow up without a solid sense of self. The resulting fragmentation may later be diagnosed Dissociative Identity Disorder (DID) or Dissociative Disorder Not Otherwise Specified (DDNOS).

Lifespan Integration therapy can be used to help a client to build a more solid self-structure and to learn to regulate emotion. Unlike talking therapies, which involve mostly the left brain hemispheres of both client and therapist, Lifespan Integration is body based. When LI is done correctly there is an exchange of energy and information between the right brain hemispheres and body-minds of therapist and client. During the Lifespan Integration Attunement protocol, this exchange is designed to replicate and replace the exchange which should have happened for the client within the mother-infant dyad from the moment of birth. New, positive feeling states are generated in the client-therapist dyad, and then are integrated as the client views the 'movie' of his life from infancy all the way into present time. A right brain to right brain connection is maintained between client and therapist throughout this re-parenting work. The success of this 're-wiring' depends on the internal coherence of the administering therapist in the same way that the attachment style of an infant is determined by the mother's coherence, her ability to attune to her child, and her ability to self-regulate.

After Lifespan Integration therapy, recipients find themselves spontaneously reacting to current stressors in more age appropriate ways. Individuals who begin LI therapy with memory gaps are eventually able to connect the pieces of their lives into a coherent whole. Clients who have completed Lifespan Integration therapy report that they feel better about their lives, are more self-accepting, and are better able to enjoy their intimate relationships.

Chapter Two
The Neurobiological Basis of Lifespan Integration

Research into brain development of infants and children has shown that some of the most important factors required for neural integration in the child are:

- a reciprocal and attuned relationship between parent and child.
- an exchange of energy and information between the minds of parent and child.
- the co-construction of the child's autobiographical narrative.
- the establishment of an internal map of self across space and time within the developing child.

Anecdotal evidence from therapists using Lifespan Integration therapy over the past ten years has shown us that the re-creation of these above conditions within the therapeutic setting encourages neural integration to take place in adult clients. Pascual-Leone and others have demonstrated that the brain does not differentiate between real and imagined experience. Our clinical evidence indicates that when the above conditions are adequately met in adulthood, through imagined experience, neural development which was incomplete or interrupted due to trauma or neglect in childhood can be completed or restored.

Effects of Trauma on Early Neural Development
Neural development is an interactive process between parent and child. Siegel (1999) tells us that "the human mind emerges from patterns in the flow of energy and information within the brain and between brains" (p.2). Schore (1994) discusses the importance of a caretaker-infant dyad in which the adult caretaker regulates the emotional states of the infant during critical developmental periods and until the infant has become capable of self-regulation. Optimal neural development in the infant and young child occurs when the parent is finely tuned to her child, and is receptive to his or her changing states and needs. When circumstances or external stressors prevent a parent from being optimally receptive and flexibly responsive to the chang-

5

ing states and needs of her developing infant, or when that parent is incapable of regulating her own emotions, neural development in the child can be impaired. "Dyadic failures of affect regulation result in the developmental psychopathology that underlies various forms of later forming psychiatric disorders" (Schore, 1994, p. 33).

In the infant or young child the self originally exists as a series of separated self-states (Siegel, 1999). When development proceeds normally, these separated self-states are integrated into a unified self. "The integrating mind attempts to create a sense of coherence among multiple selves across time and across contexts." (Siegel, 1999, p. 315). How this happens is still not fully understood. Neuroscientists believe it involves the co-construction of the autobiographical narrative between parent and child. "The co-construction of narratives drives the integration of cognition, affect, sensation, and behaviors." (Cozolino, 2002, p. 263.)

Difficulties with affect tolerance and affect regulation may be related to failures in neural integration during developmental periods. Schore (1994) suggests that:

> The mother's external regulation of the infant's developing yet still immature emotional systems during particular critical periods may represent the essential factor that influences the experience-dependent growth of brain areas prospectively involved in self-regulation. (pp. 31-32)

Schore goes on to say:

> The core of the self lies in patterns of affect regulation that integrate a sense of self across state transitions, thereby allowing for a continuity of inner experience. (p.33)

Traumatic experiences which impact children during early development can have profound and lasting effects. Because the mind develops interactively with the environment, trauma in childhood can affect how the individual views the world for the rest of his life. Critical to how a child responds to trauma neurologically is the ability of the parent or adult caretaker to mediate the experience of trauma for the child.

Certain suboptimal attachment experiences produce multiple, incoherent working models of attachment and engrained and inflexible states of mind that remain un-integrated across time within specialized and potentially dysfunctional self-states. (Siegel, 1999, p. 306)

Traumatic experiences are all the more damaging if the perpetrator happens to be a family member. Children often dissociate during traumatic incidents, and later in life they may lack explicit memories of what they experienced as children. However the trauma remains stored in the body-mind as implicit memory. Siegel (1999) writes:

With dissociation or the prohibition of discussing with others what was experienced, as is so often the case in familial child abuse, there may be a profound blockage to the pathway toward consolidating memory. Unresolved traumatic experiences from this perspective may involve an impairment in the cortical consolidation process, which leaves the memories of these events out of permanent memory. But the person may be prone to experiencing continually intrusive implicit images of past horrors. (p. 52)

We now know that the co-construction of autobiographical narratives is an important component of neural integration. When a child has no one with whom he or she can discuss a traumatic incident, it is likely that, without intervention, the implicit memory of the trauma will be held in a separated ego state throughout the lifespan. Cozolino (2002) points out that:

Early abuse may not only correlate with the lack of assistance of caretakers in the co-construction of coherent narratives about the self, it may also result in damage to neural structures required to organize cohesive narratives and the story of the self that will persist into adult life. (p.256)

Until recently the prevailing view among neuroscientists was that the brain develops beginning shortly after conception and continuing throughout childhood. It was thought that once this developmental process was complete, there would be no further synaptic growth and certainly no possiblility of ongoing neurogenesis.

Now there is no question that the brain remodels itself throughout life, and that it retains the capacity to change itself as the result not only of passively experienced factors such as enriched environments, but also of changes in the ways we behave (taking up the violin) and the ways we think. (Schwartz & Begley, 2002, pp.253-254)

There is now ample evidence not only of brain plasticity but of the capacity of the cerebral cortex to reorganize itself. Neural networks are not static, but rather dynamic and changing. Changes in our experiences correlate with changes in our neural circuitry, however neural change is more likely to occur when we are attending to our experience and when we are emotionally engaged.

Implicit Memories Affect Adults in the Present
Adults who experienced or witnessed overwhelming and terrifying events when they were children, and who did not have adequate parental protection and support available, may or may not have explicit memories of what happened to them. They will, however, have implicit memories of these events stored in their body-mind systems. When implicit memories are triggered in the present, the individual 'remembers', but has no awareness that s/he is remembering anything. Along with the implicit memory, s/he may experience impulses to react defensively. These impulses may be experienced outside of conscious awareness, i.e. physiologically or somatically.

The outcome for a victim who dissociates explicit from implicit processing is an impairment in autobiographical memory for at least certain aspects of the trauma. Implicit memory of the event is intact and includes intrusive elements such as behavioral impulses to flee, emotional reactions, bodily sensations, and intrusive images related to the trauma. (Siegel, 1999, p. 51)

How the traumatized child interprets what happened, i.e. the mental schema he or she uses to make sense of the trauma, may be ultimately even more destructive to the child's emerging sense of self than was the trauma itself. The child's interpretation is dependent upon: 1) the age and developmental stage of the child at the time of the traumatic event, and 2) the amount of emotional support and factual information which was available at the time of or soon after the traumatic event (usually from a loving and supportive adult), which could help the child make sense of the event.

> Early attachment experiences organize lasting schemas (within hidden layers) which, in turn, shape our experience of those around us throughout life. The degree of integration between verbal and emotional networks will determine whether or not we become aware of our emotions or can put them into words.
> (Cozolino,2002, p.162)

We know that with trauma and PTSD, self-states remain frozen at the time of the trauma. When those states are triggered through activation of implicit memories, the individual feels as though he or she is re-experiencing the trauma in the present.

Thanks to recent research in neuroscience, we now have a better understanding of early neural development and of how various factors in childhood can affect development in ways which lead to later psychological problems. We also have new information at hand telling us that the brain continues to reorganize itself throughout the lifespan. This new knowledge presents new opportunities for psychotherapists. We can now ask ourselves: "When working with adults who were traumatized during developmental stages, how can we best help them to repair neural systems that were damaged? How can we help them to integrate neural networks that remain isolated from one another?" To answer these questions it makes sense to study what is known to date about neural integration. Neural integration is an important feature of development, and lack of integration is at the root of a multitude of problems including problems with relationships, response flexibility, the ability to construct a coherent autobiographical narrative, and the ability to adequately parent (Siegel 1999).

Factors which Contribute to Neural Integration

As mentioned earlier, the self begins as a series of separated self-states. How these separated self-states become an integrated whole is a current topic of interest and speculation among neuroscientists. Following are some statements which partially summarize the most recent thinking regarding neural integration:

- "A number of authors propose that the associational areas of the neocortex, such as the prefrontal regions (including the orbitofrontal cortex) that link various widely distributed representational processes together, form dynamic global maps or complex representations from the input of widely distributed regions in order to establish a sensorimotor integration of the self across space and time." (Siegel, 1999, p. 330).

- LeDoux (2002) proposes that our brains make us who we are by way of "synaptic processes that allow cooperative interactions to take place between the various brain systems that are involved in particular states and experiences, and for these interactions to be linked over time" (p. 32).

- Damasio (1994) suggests that our sense of an integrated mind is a result of various neural networks being synchronized through a "trick of timing." "If activity occurs in anatomically separate brain regions, but if it does so within approximately the same window of time, it is still possible to link the parts behind the scenes, as it were, and create the impression that it all happens in the same place" (p. 95).

- "The capacity for self-integration, like the processes of the mind itself, is continually created by an interaction of internal neurophysiological processes and interpersonal relationships." (Siegel, 1999, p. 314).

- "Co-constructed narratives in an emotionally supportive environment can provide the necessary matrix for the psychological and neurobiological integration required to avoid dissociative reactions." (Cozolino, 2002, p. 26

According to the above authors and thinkers, some of the important components of neural integration are:

- The creation of a global map of self across space and time.
- The co-construction of autobiographical narratives.
- Linking self-states across space and time within an emotionally supportive interpersonal relationship.
- Cooperation between brain systems which are involved in various states and experiences, and linking these interactions through time.

More Changes Occur under Conditions of Neural Plasticity

Neural plasticity is the condition which exists when many neurons are firing at the same time. More neurons firing increases the likelihood that new synaptic firing patterns will occur. Both new learning, and changes in old patterns are more likely to occur under conditions of neural plasticity.

Intervening to Help Ego States Who Are Stuck in the Past

During Lifespan Integration processing, the therapist reaches out to the child ego state in the memory scene (who is frozen in the past) through the adult client who holds this and other ego states as part of her neural landscape. The therapist instructs the adult client to enter into an internal dialogue with the targeted child ego state. The therapist, through the adult client, brings support and information to the ego state in the past, and encourages this child ego state to re-interpret the past experience based on the new information. The conversation with the child ego state is interactive. By asking the child what holds her in the past and what distresses her, it is possible to discover how the child has interpreted the traumatic event, i.e. what negative cognitions about herself the child may be holding and/or what she is having trouble letting go of. The interaction with the child ego state may also include imaginally holding the child, rocking her, or taking her for or a bike ride or on a camping trip.

The therapist structures his interventions with the child in the past based on his knowledge of child development, his knowledge of the particular traumatic event being targeted, the available family history of the adult client, and the information (feedback) that he is receiving from the child ego state as reported to him by his adult client. "Stage-appropriate attunement and scaffolding of basic functions will maximize neural growth and network coherence. For the newborn, this may be reflected in stroking and cuddling; in a four-year-old, it means helping him or her to learn to share with a sibling." (Cozolino, 2002, pp. 191-192). In Lifespan Integration processing, this stage-appropriate internal conversation and interaction between adult and child, followed by 'traveling' visually through time to the present, is usually repeated three to five or more times for each source memory. The details of the internal conversation and/or imaginal interaction with the child may vary during the repetitions, depending on the feedback which the therapist and adult client receive from the child ego state.

Use of Imagery and Active Imagination

Lifespan Integration approaches the construction of the autobiographical narrative through the use of imagery rather than through the use of a verbal narrative. In addition to constructing the map of self across space-time, Lifespan Integration uses active imagination to intervene in the past to: 1) repair early life experiences, and 2) to insert positive imaginal interactions with a new attachment figure (the client's adult self). Reconstructing the past in this way can create positive and lasting change in the present. LeDoux (2002) writes:

> If a thought is embodied as a pattern of synaptic transmission within a network of brain cells, as must be the case, then it stands to reason that the brain activity that is a thought can influence activity in other brain systems involved in perception, motivation, movement, and the like. But there's one more connection to make. If a thought is a pattern of neural activity in a network, not only can it cause another network to be active, it can also cause another network to change, to be plastic. (p. 319.)

Research done in 1995 by Pascual-Leone demonstrated that imagined movements created changes in neural networks to the same degree that actual physical movements did. "Like actual, physical movements, imagined movements trigger synaptic change at the cortical level. Merely thinking about moving produced brain changes comparable to those triggered by actually moving" (Schwartz & Begley, 2002, p. 217). Recent research thus validates what those of us who have used imagery for healing trauma have known intuitively and from our experience working with clients. Imaginal interventions in past traumas change how those traumas affect clients in the present.

Images existed before words, and are the precursors to language. (Damasio, 1994, pp.106-107). "Mental images and bodily sensations are the building blocks of the internal representation of the self. The construction of inner imaginal space creates the possibility for perspective and empathy for others as well as for ourselves." (Cozolino, 2002, p. 148). Images in the human mind could be compared to a computer's operating system or basic language. The mind's ability to put images into words could be likened to a program such as Window's "Word" which is able to perform a more complex function only with the help of the computer's underlying basic language.

Importance of Repetition

During Lifespan Integration processing, the client is grounded in his bodily sensations as he brings up images of himself participating in scenes from his life, year by year, across time. Each repetition through the Time Line of memories and images reinforces the client's sense of himself across time. Each repetition also incorporates more and more memories. These repetitions of the Time Line require multiple and repeated state shifts. Repetitions of state transitions help to organize and stabilize the self system. Repetitions of the Time Line also help to strengthen the newly created synaptic connections, increasing the chances that they will fire in the same pattern again and again. Schwartz & Begley (2002) explain in detail how learning takes place at the synaptic level:

> Hebbian plasticity begins with the release from presynaptic neurons of the neurotransmitter, glutamate. The glutamate binds to two kinds of receptors on the postsynaptic neuron. One receptor notes that its own neuron, the postsynaptic one is active; the other notes which presynaptic neurons are simultaneously active. The postsynaptic neuron therefore detects the simultaneous occurrence of presynaptic and postsynaptic activity. The ultimate result is that a particular action potential whizzing down the axon of a presynaptic neuron becomes more efficient at causing the postsynaptic neuron to fire. When that happens, we say that there has been an increase in synaptic strength. The two neurons thus become locked in a physiological embrace,

allowing the formation of functional circuits during gestation and childhood. The process is analogous to the way that traveling the same dirt road over and over leaves ruts that make it easier to stay in the track on subsequent trips. Similarly, stimulating the same chain of neurons over and over—as when a child memorizes what a cardinal looks like—increases the chances that the circuit will fire all the way through to completion, until the final action potential stimulates the neuron in the language centers, and allows the kid to blurt out "Cardinal!" (pp.107-108)

Repeated visual and sensual journeys through time during Lifespan Integration can likewise be compared to traveling the same dirt road over and over. The newly formed synaptic pathways linking past to present become strengthened, eventually creating 'grooves' that are easy to follow.

Lifespan Integration Re-Organizes the Self System

Lifespan Integration therapy is based on the hypothesis that much psychological dysfunction results from insufficient neural organization. Due to trauma or neglect experienced during childhood, there may be a lack of connectivity between isolated neural networks which represent separate selves and self-states. Alternatively, problems could be caused by suboptimal integration between various regions and layers of the brain.

Through the process of repetitions of the LI Time Line, the self system becomes increasingly more and better organized both in space and in time. This increase in organization occurs in part due to the many shifts between selves and self-states which are required by repetitions of the LI Time Line. With repetitions of the Time Line, transitions between self-states become more fluid. This fluidity also contributes to the stability of the self-system.

The stability of a system is dependent upon its capacity to transition between and thereby exist within a range of possible states...(Schore, 2003, p. 93)

These shifts between multitudinous self states are made in the presence of a therapist whose calm and steady presence aids the client with emotional regulation and containment throughout

14

the process. The therapist's body-mind coherence is transmitted to the client in the same way that a parent transmits coherence (or lack thereof) to her child.

After several repetitions of the Time Line of memories and images, the shifting between states becomes more fluid. Likewise, the client's autobiographical narrative becomes better organized and more coherent. The client begins to see himself as existing throughout a continuum of time and space. The client's memories begin to flow from one year to the next, becoming more inclusive with each repetition. The memories which surface spontaneously in this process will share the feeling tone of the targeted trauma. By following this emotional theme through time, the client gains insights about the defensive systems he has employed, and the patterns he has played out as a result of his interpretations of emotionally impactful events. From this detached state of awareness, the client is able and willing to drop archaic defenses, and to adopt new and more adaptive strategies.

Through the process of repetitions of the Time Line of memories and images, the client creates a global map of himself which spans time and space. Once this neural map is in place, the client is able to move through state transitions fluidly, and his memories become more organized across time. Once an individual has developed a neurological map of self that allows him to see himself as existing continuously throughout his entire lifespan, it is no longer possible for that individual to become frozen in time or even to be triggered by an implicit memory.

Outcomes Indicate Evidence of Change at the Synaptic Level
Clients who have completed Lifespan Integration therapy report:

- A newfound sense of a competent, capable, lovable, and solid self.
- The ability to let go of archaic defensive strategies.
- An enhanced ability to enjoy life and intimate relationships.
- A much improved ability to regulate affect.
- An expanded emotional repertoire.

Summary

In Lifespan Integration therapy the therapist and client in effect co-construct the client's life narrative. During this process, the therapist stays attuned to the client while reading the client's memory cues. As the client 'views' past scenes he re-experiences memories in chronological order, leading to increased integration and a more solid self structure. Repeated chronological excursions through time in the presence of an emotionally available and profoundly attuned therapist allow the client to create coherence among selves and self-states across time and across contexts.

As the client repeatedly views the 'movie' of his life, more positive memories and insights will begin to emerge. Neural plasticity is enhanced through the client's optimal emotional engagement as he 'views' his life. The client's ability to stay optimally emotionally engaged is facilitated by the therapist's containment and attunement. Neural plasticity is also enhanced as the client's attention stays focused on the memory images of his life including the accompanying smells, sounds, and bodily sensations which correspond to his changing emotional states. Due to the repetitive nature of the process, the new firing patterns between neurons and neural networks are reinforced.

Chapter Three

Applied Neuroscience
Hows and Whys of Lifespan Integration

Emotion Affects Encoding of Memory

When children experience overwhelming and terrifying events, explicit memories of these terrifying events are not encoded. Children are extremely resilient, and if adult support is available to help them make sense of what they have experienced, they are able to integrate these experiences and move forward with their lives relatively unscathed. Adults who survived or witnessed overwhelming and terrifying events in childhood, without an emotionally available adult present to help them make sense of and integrate these traumatic experiences, will carry the implicit memories of these traumatic events in their body-mind systems, without explicit recollection of what happened. Later in life, when the adult recalls the event, he has no autobiographical context for what he is feeling, and he may not even realize that he is recalling an actual event. The emotions, impulses, and bodily sensations which arise in the individual when an implicit memory has been triggered, seem to come out of nowhere.

Lifespan Integration Differs from Traditional Therapeutic Methods

In the past we were taught that an important aspect of therapy is emotional release, that clients needed to grieve their losses, and that "getting it all out" (emoting) during therapy was part of the healing process. Recent research has overturned that antiquated way of thinking. Siegel (1999) gives us a new way to think of emotion:

> Let us assume that the familiar end products of emotion— what we usually consider in everyday thinking as the common feelings of anger, fear, sadness, or joy—are actually *not* central to the initial experience of emotion. Let us also assume that emotions do not necessarily exist at all as we usually think of them: as some kind of packets of something that can be experienced, identified, and expressed, as implied in the statement 'Just get your feelings out.' Instead, let's consider that *emotions represent dynamic processes created within the socially influenced, value-appraising processes of the brain.* (p. 123.)

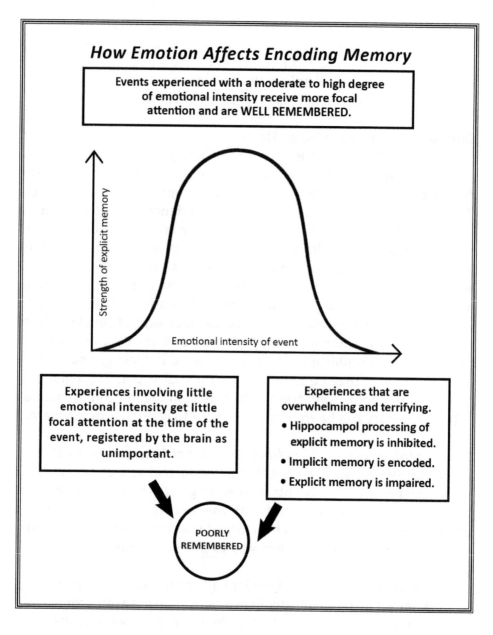

How Emotion Affects Encoding Memory

Events experienced with a moderate to high degree of emotional intensity receive more focal attention and are WELL REMEMBERED.

Strength of explicit memory

Emotional intensity of event

Experiences involving little emotional intensity get little focal attention at the time of the event, registered by the brain as unimportant.

Experiences that are overwhelming and terrifying.

• Hippocampol processing of explicit memory is inhibited.

• Implicit memory is encoded.

• Explicit memory is impaired.

POORLY REMEMBERED

Diagram 1

When using Lifespan Integration therapy, emotion-laden memories need to be visited only briefly, for the purpose of 'hooking into' the relevant neural circuitry. Revisiting traumatic memories simply for the purpose of releasing emotion is not necessary or helpful in the healing process. If emotions result from a particular alignment of neural networks firing together, then repeated revisiting of traumatic memories which are represented by these networks will only serve to reinforce the related emotional responses. Peter Levine (1997), in talking about his work with traumatized clients writes:

> I learned that it was unnecessary to dredge up old memories and relive their emotional pain to heal trauma. In fact, severe emotional pain can be re-traumatizing. What we need to do to be freed from our symptoms and fears is to arouse our deep physiological resources and consciously utilize them. If we remain ignorant of our power to change the course of our instinctual responses in a proactive rather than reactive way, we will continue being imprisoned and in pain. (p.31)

With Lifespan Integration processing, the way to be freed from this emotional pain is to move quickly through the memories as they come up. When moving through the Time Line, the memories are viewed in rapid succession, without leaving time for discussion or for 'emotional release'. The Lifespan Integration method follows the client's body-mind system back and forth through TIME in an effort to connect implicit memories to the actual events from which they stem. Repetitions of these journeys through TIME are the integrating factor in Lifespan Integration therapy.

Importance of Relationship

Neural development is an interactive process between parent and child. Siegel (1999) tells us that "the human mind emerges from patterns in the flow of energy and information within the brain and between brains" (p.2). Schore (1994) discusses the importance of a caretaker-infant dyad in which the adult caretaker regulates the emotional states of the infant during critical developmental periods and until the infant has become capable of self-regulation. He goes on to say: "Dyadic failures of affect regulation result in the developmental

19

psychopathology that underlies various forms of later forming psychiatric disorders" (Schore, 1994, p. 33).

In Lifespan Integration therapy, the therapist (in effect) takes on the role which the parent or caregiver normally provides in early development. Energy and information are exchanged between the therapist's body-mind system and the client's body-mind system. The therapist, simply by her presence, acts as a container and regulator of the client's emotions. Presence is key to good results. The therapist must remain present, grounded, energetically connected to the client, and emotionally available throughout the process. When using Lifespan Integration as a therapeutic method, therapists who have done their own work toward integrating their own self systems will get better results with their clients than those therapists who have not done sufficient body-mind therapy to heal their own early neglect or trauma.

State Transitions across Time

Linking states across time is an important component of neural integration. Making repeated journeys through the Lifespan Integration Time Line requires the client to continually transition from state to state. These transitions along the continuum of time allow various self states and feeling states to become better organized. As the self system becomes more organized, it also becomes more stable. "As the patterns of relations among the components of a self-organizing system become increasingly interconnected and well-ordered, it is more capable of maintaining a coherence or organization in relation to variations in the environment." (Schore, 2003, p. 93). With repetitions of the Time Line, state transitions become more fluid. This fluidity also contributes to the stability of the self system.

Importance of Repetition

During Lifespan Integration processing, to the degree that the client is grounded in his body, he will re-experience the smells, sounds, and tactile sensations associated with each memory image. Each repetition of the Time Line of memories and images reinforces the client's sense of himself across time. Each repetition also incorporates more and more memories. These repetitions of the Time Line require multiple and repeated state shifts. Repetitions of state transitions help to organize and stabilize the self system. Repetitions of the Time Line also help to strengthen the newly created synaptic connections, increasing the chances that they will fire in the same pattern again and again.

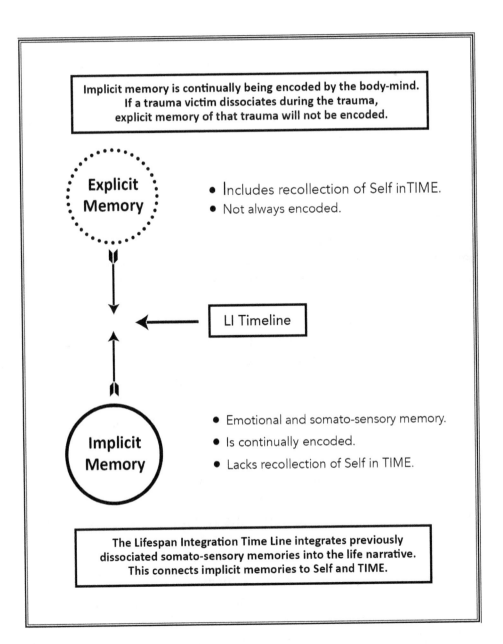

Implicit memory is continually being encoded by the body-mind.
If a trauma victim dissociates during the trauma,
explicit memory of that trauma will not be encoded.

Explicit Memory

- Includes recollection of Self in TIME.
- Not always encoded.

LI Timeline

- Emotional and somato-sensory memory.
- Is continually encoded.
- Lacks recollection of Self in TIME.

Implicit Memory

The Lifespan Integration Time Line integrates previously
dissociated somato-sensory memories into the life narrative.
This connects implicit memories to Self and TIME.

Diagram 2

Attention Enhances Neural Plasticity.

Recent research has shown that synaptic changes are more likely to happen when attention is focused. "Passive, unattended, or little-attended exercises are of limited value...Plastic changes in brain representations are generated only when behaviors are specifically attended." (Schwartz & Begley, 2002, p.224, quoting Merzenich and Jenkins.)

Emotion Enhances Neural Plasticity.

Neural networks are more plastic when subjects are emotionally aroused. Research has shown us that learning and memory are enhanced when subjects are optimally emotionally engaged. LeDoux (2002) describes how emotions contribute to neural plasticity.

> "(B)ecause more brain systems are typically active during emotional than during nonemotional states, and the intensity of arousal is greater, the opportunity for coordinated learning across brain systems is greater during emotional states. By coordinating parallel plasticity throughout the brain, emotional states promote the development and unification of the self" (p 322).

Extremely intense emotional states overwhelm the system and cause flooding or dissociation. Re-experiencing the intense emotions of a past trauma can re-traumatize the system, and does not contribute to healing.

Autobiographical Narratives and Attachment Research

In the 1950's, Mary Ainsworth, a pioneer in attachment research, studied mother-infant interactions over the infants' first year of life. Ainsworth developed an assessment tool: "The Strange Situation." Using this tool she measured and described four different attachment styles in children: secure, avoidant, resistant or ambivalent, and disorganized/disoriented.

In the early 1980's Mary Main and Ruth Goldwyn extended attachment studies, and created a new measurement tool: the Adult Attachment Interview, or AAI. In the AAI the adult is asked to relate an autobiographical narrative about his or her childhood. This narrative is to include a description of his or her early relationships with each parent,

Normal Development and Secure Attachment

Parent figure has been available to child for Co-construction of child's autobiographical life narrative. Map of self across space and time is in place. Neural activity is sufficient for mental health.

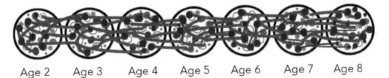

Age 2   Age 3   Age 4   Age 5   Age 6   Age 7   Age 8

Dissociation / Memory Gaps

History of trauma. Parent figure(s) either non-supportive or unavailable. Autobiographical narrative is only partially constructed. Map of self across space and time is incomplete.

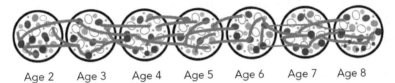

Age 2   Age 3   Age 4   Age 5   Age 6   Age 7   Age 8

Dissociative Identity Disorder

History of overwhelming trauma with little or no parental support available. Autobiographical narrative has not been constructed. Map of self across space and time is extremely sketchy. Neural integration is minimal.

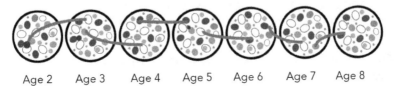

Age 2   Age 3   Age 4   Age 5   Age 6   Age 7   Age 8

In this model, the small circles within the larger circles represent separated neural networks which are held within the body-mind system. The lines connecting the dots represent neural pathways created by synaptic connections between neural networks.

Diagram 3

and how these relationships changed over time. The AAI is then scored for how well the adult is able to present and evaluate his or her childhood experience to the interviewer. When scoring the AAI, the rater looks at: the balance between factual material and emotional content; the relevance of examples used; and the plausibility, consistency, clarity, and coherence of the narrative.

Main and Goldwyn found that the AAI score attained by a parent or parent-to-be predicts with 75% to 85% accuracy the attachment pattern which children born to this parent will express in the parent-child dyad. The AAI predicts attachment accurately even when the children are not yet born. The more balanced, relevant, and coherent the autobiographical narrative of the adult, the more likely his child will form a secure attachment.

These findings suggest that an adult who has made sense of both his childhood experiences and his early relationship with his parents is able to be emotionally available and fully present for his own child, meeting the conditions for the child's neural integration to proceed optimally.

Autonoetic Consciousness

The ability to see the self across time is called autonoetic consciousness. "Autobiographical or episodic memory requires a capacity termed 'autonoesis' (self-knowing) and appears to be dependent upon the development of frontal cortical regions of the brain." (Siegel, 1999, p. 35). Siegel suggests that "the capacity of the mind to create such a global map of the self across time and various contexts—to have autonoetic consciousness—is an essential feature of integration that may continue to develop throughout life" (1999, p. 330).

Lifespan Integration Promotes Neural Integration

Step 1 of LI standard protocol follows the affect bridge within the client's body-mind system to uncover/discover the poorly integrated past neural networks most connected to present distress or dysfunction. (See Diagram 4.)

Steps 2 through 5 are all important for setting up the conditions so that optimal neural integration can occur in Step 6, through repetitions of the Time Line. The conditions which are met in steps 2 through 5 are:

- Relationship to a grounded and emotionally available other,
- Focused attention, and
- Connection to bodily sensation of emotion.

When the adult self of the client imaginally enters the scene, she takes the child to a peaceful place and discusses the past event with the child, bringing in new information and reframing what happened. Sometimes the adult self expresses anger on behalf of the child before taking the child to the peaceful place. The therapist coaches the adult self to intervene in the past scene in whatever way is needed to give the child self a felt sense of safety. If the child self does not feel safe, she will not be able to give her attention to the process.

During the internal conversation, current information is brought to the child state, however it is not necessary to convince the child of the changes in the child's 'reality,' or the truth of the new information. When either therapist or adult client persists in arguing with the

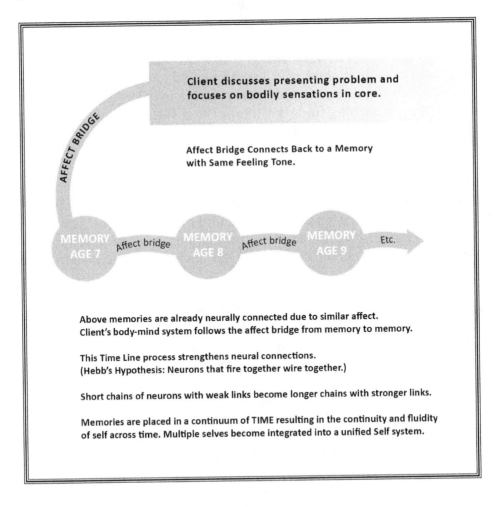

Diagram 4

child self, valuable session time is wasted which could be used more productively by going through repetitions of the Time Line. In addition, arguing with the child can disrupt the emotional bond between the adult and child, and can cause the child self to stop attending to the process. When the child's comments show that she does not believe the new information, the therapist instructs the adult client to say to her: "I can understand why you would think that/feel that way. Let me show you how you have grown up and become an important part of me and how things are different now." Then go to Step 6, the Time Line. After sufficient repetitions of Steps 3-7, the child state will be integrated into the self system, and all of the information held by the self system will be available to the child self.

The therapist never speaks directly to the child self, but instead feeds his interventions to the inner child through the adult client. (See Diagram 5). When the adult client is in her feelings, in her body, and deeply connected to her child state, she truly doesn't know what her child self needs to hear. This is true even if the adult client is—in real time—a skilled child psychotherapist. If the therapist were to ask the adult client to enter into conversation with the child ego state, (i.e., without coaching from the therapist) it would be necessary for the adult client to leave the child ego state and enter into a more cognitive mode. Integration occurs only to the degree that clients are able to stay grounded and connected to their bodily sensations and past states. The best way to keep the client's connection with her child self intact is to keep the client away from cognitive activities (thinking) as much as possible. At the end of the protocol, and when back in present time, the adult client is given an opportunity to continue the internal conversation with her child self without help from the therapist.

Neural Integration occurs in Step 6 of the Lifespan Integration protocol. During Step 6 the therapist leads the client chronologically through her life, asking the client to view the memories or images which spontaneously come up for each year of her life. This process provides the following remaining components:

- Co-construction of the autobiographical narrative, and
- Repetitions of state transitions across time.

To ensure integration, Steps 3-7 should be repeated three to five or more times, or until the internal conversation in present time (Step 7) shows that the child self is 100% convinced that the past is over. When integration is complete, viewing the past scene (source memory) will no longer produce a bodily sensation of emotion in the client.

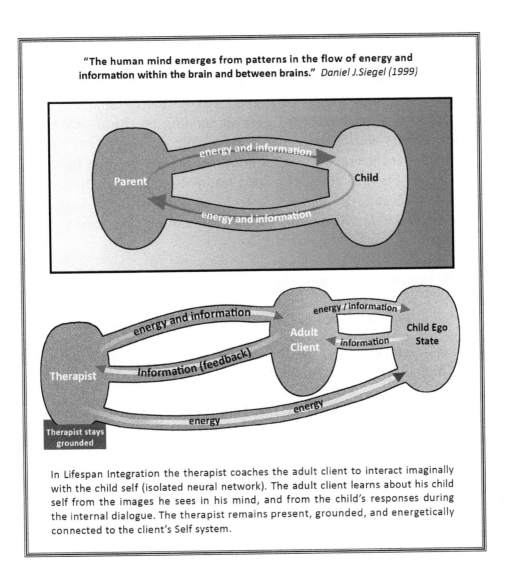

"The human mind emerges from patterns in the flow of energy and information within the brain and between brains." *Daniel J.Siegel (1999)*

Parent

energy and information

Child

energy and information

energy and information

Adult Client

energy / information

Child Ego State

information

Therapist

Information (feedback)

energy

energy

Therapist stays grounded

In Lifespan Integration the therapist coaches the adult client to interact imaginally with the child self (isolated neural network). The adult client learns about his child self from the images he sees in his mind, and from the child's responses during the internal dialogue. The therapist remains present, grounded, and energetically connected to the client's Self system.

Diagram 5

Through repetitions of the Time Line of memories and images, the client creates a global map of herself which spans time and space. Once this neural map is in place, the client is able to move through state transitions fluidly, and her memories become more organized across time.

Making repeated journeys through the Lifespan Integration Time Line requires the client to continually transition from state to state. These transitions along the continuum of time allow various self-states and feeling states to become more organized. As implicit memories become associated with actual historical events, the client's body-mind system is able to reorganize itself, storing these bodily and somatic states more appropriately as memories of past events. As the self system becomes more organized, it also becomes more stable.

Different LI protocols are used depending on the needs of the client. Clients whose early needs were adequately met can benefit from standard protocol LI. Standard protocol can be used for a presenting problem or to clear a past traumatic memory. Clients who experienced early trauma or neglect will need to begin LI therapy with several sessions of the Lifespan Integration structure building protocols.

About the Lifespan Integration Time Line

- The Time Line is the key component of Lifespan Integration.

- Repetitions of the Time Line integrate new feeling states and allow the body to understand the passage of time.

- Through repetitions of the Time Line the client creates coherence among selves and self-states across time and across contexts.

- A space-time map of self is created. A neural map of self across space and time is necessary for spatio-temporal integration.

- Through repetitions of the Time Line of images in the presence of an attuned therapist, the client in effect co-constructs his autobiographical narrative.

- More memories are 'remembered' and integrated during each subsequent journey through the Time Line.

- This process 'presents' the client with a panoramic view of his life across space and time. The client is thus able to see the patterns in decisions and choices he has made throughout his lifespan. The client is able to see how he has defended himself throughout his life against the perceived danger of the earlier trauma. He 'sees' that he is safe to make other choices now.

The process of navigating through the Lifespan Integration Time Line requires the client to access chronological information and facts from the left brain hemisphere, and to retrieve images and emotional memories from the right brain hemisphere.

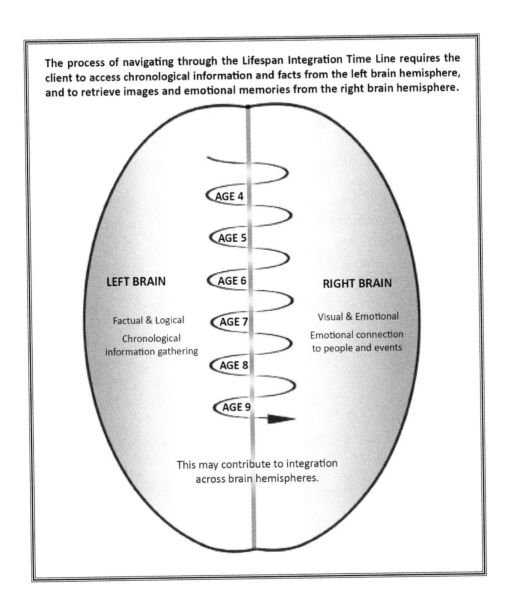

Diagram 6

- The ratio of positive to negative memories increases with each subsequent journey through the Time Line. (More positive memories come up with each repetition.) This is true for all clients. *Note: Some clients will initially unconsciously guard against or censor their most unpleasant memories. When this happens the memories may appear to get worse during the first few repetitions. As the client begins to relax and trust the process, she will stop censoring the images. Once the client connects to the most difficult memories, more positive images will surface with each repetition.*

Model of Isolated Neural Networks

When children experience overwhelming or terrifying events without the support of emotionally available caregivers, they develop many isolated neural networks (self states). These self states are linked to implicit memories. They are loosely associated to one another through common affect, but they are not integrated into the Self system, nor are they anchored in a chronological time frame. In the model below, the small circles represent neural networks which are held within the body-mind, but are not integrated into the whole Self system.

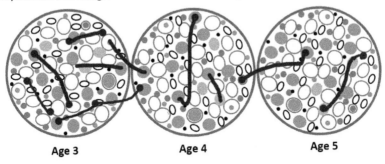

Age 3   Age 4   Age 5

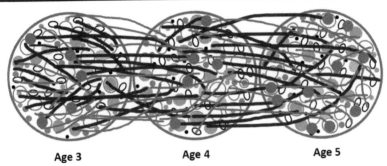

Age 3   Age 4   Age 5

Model of How Lifespan Integration Links Memories through Time to Create a More Coherent Self System

Lifespan Integration begins with a series of isolated neural networks which are loosely associated by a common affect, and links them together across time. Events throughout the lifespan which share a common emotion are linked together chronologically by following the affect bridge through time, year by year, from one memory to another, and all the way into present time.

Diagram 7

Chapter Four
Lifespan Integration Standard Protocol

This chapter is descriptive rather than instructive. It is recommended that therapists attend an approved Lifespan Integration training before attempting to use this method. LI is an extremely powerful and effective therapy. When LI therapy is done correctly, the client's unconscious contents are 'stirred up', re-arranged, and integrated all within a 60 or 90 minute session. An inexperienced and untrained therapist attempting this method may activate a client's material without fully integrating it. Doing LI only partly right may not help the client, and could possibly harm him.

Preparing Clients for Lifespan Integration Therapy:

- Explain to the client that Lifespan Integration is most likely very different from any type of therapy she may have experienced in the past. Explain that LI works on the body-mind system, and give a brief overview of how a typical LI session works.

- Explain to the client the importance of allowing spontaneous images to come up when traveling through the Time Line of memories and images. If the process is working correctly, some new and different images will surface spontaneously on each subsequent journey through the Time Line.

- Explain to the client the necessity of repeating the Time Line of memories and images until positive memories or insights begin to spontaneously emerge.

- Explain to the client that it is necessary to stay grounded in her body and to keep her attention focused on both the memory images and the bodily sensations related to the memories and images which come up.

- Explain to the client that there is no need to talk about the memories which come up when going through the Time Line, and that it is not necessary to spend time exploring each image. What works best is to 'watch the movie' and move quickly from scene to scene.

- Explain to the client that Lifespan Integration therapy allows the body-mind to heal itself. The healing will not be complete for 24 to 48 hours after the session. The client may feel a little spacey for several hours after the session. A small percentage of clients have trouble sleeping after experiencing Lifespan Integration. When this happens it is only temporary and is a result of the ongoing processing in the client's body-mind.

Preparing the Memory Cue List

When first beginning to do Lifespan Integration therapy, many people are unable to get a spontaneous flow of memories during the Time Line step of the LI protocol. Even people who have fluid memory recall for most years of their lives may have some gaps or stretches of years where memories are much harder to access. Memory cues serve as markers in time which allow the person remembering to remain in his right brain hemisphere. Each time the same cue is read on subsequent repetitions, other related memories will surface. With increased integration the client moves toward a more free association of memories as he goes from year to year visually.

Some clients can write their memory cue lists without help from the therapist. Clients with traumatic histories may prefer to write their cues with help from the therapist. The cues should be completed prior to beginning Lifespan Integration therapy. For some clients with memory gaps this may take a few sessions. The memory cue list should have at least one memory for each year of the client's life. One memory cue per year is adequate, but for variation it is useful to have two or three per year. Significant events such as marriages, divorces, deaths, and births should be included. Each cue should be specific to a particular time frame. Each cue should be an event which the client actually remembers. The cues can be scenes from photographs, but only if the client actually remembers experiencing the event which was captured in the photograph.

The memories do not need to be significant in any way. Even remembering what a house or school building looked like is enough detail for these memory aids. Trips taken, names of friends, various work places or living spaces all work well for memory cues. The memory cues can be changed during the course of LI therapy. There is no advantage in continuing to use the same cues session after session. After a few sessions, the therapist may give the client the opportunity to write a new, improved, cue list.

Cues allow the client to relax and enjoy a right brain process. The cues will not limit the surfacing of other spontaneous memories from that same time frame, but rather cues will enhance the process of spontaneous memory retrieval. Use the memory cues that the client brings to the session, even if the cues are mostly about various traumas throughout the lifespan. Traumatic memories are the most indelible and therefore are best remembered. An experienced and attuned LI therapist can use a traumatic cue list to bring the client through time without activating the cued trauma memories. Inexperienced LI therapists should wait until they have more experience, and should get supervision from an approved LI consultant if working with a client whose cues are mostly traumatic.

Memory Expansion Indicates Integration

Neural integration is occurring when the client reports that spontaneous memories are surfacing, and that these memories vary with each repetition of Step 6, the LI Time Line. If clients report that they consistently have the same memories coming up on each repetition, neural integration is not occurring during the TL. The most likely reason for this is that the client is using a left brain process to retrieve memories. If a client seems to be thinking too much, or using a left brain process to retrieve memories, read the same memory cue for each year on each repetition. Use memory cues which are more likely to hold sensory components. Very dissociative clients are often quite able to get visuals of their memories without the associated bodily sensations of emotion. Clients more present in their bodies will 'see' the memory from their perspective at the time of the memory. i.e. they will 'see' from the eyes of their child self. Embodied clients will also often remember smells, tactile sensations, or sounds associated with each memory.

Follow the Client's Body-Mind System

The human body-mind is a self-healing organism. Lifespan Integration is a healing method which follows the client's body-mind system and respects the knowledge inherent in that system. After having conducted thousands of Lifespan Integration sessions over the past ten years, I have learned to trust the client's body-mind. The client's self-system knows much better than I do where it needs to go to heal itself. Where the system goes is almost never where my analytical mind thinks it needs to go, and likewise the client's system rarely goes to where the client believes the problem originated.

When the Early History is Traumatic or Unknown

If the defensive structure underlying the client's presenting problem originated in the client's body-mind before the client was capable of encoding explicit memory, the client will not be able to retrieve a connected source memory in Step 1 of the standard LI protocol. For cases where trauma or neglect occurred prior to age two, and/or for cases where the early history is unknown, the therapist should begin with the Lifespan Integration protocols which strengthen the self and improve the client's ability to regulate emotion. (For information about the LI protocols which begin at the beginning of life, see Chapter 5.) The earlier, more primitive defenses such as splitting typically develop before a child is two years of age. When Lifespan Integration therapy is used to heal clients diagnosed with Borderline and Narcissistic Personality Disorders, the LI structure building protocols can be used to address the Borderline's splitting, and to repair the Narcissist's empty core Self. Clients who present with attachment disorders will also benefit from beginning with the LI Attunement protocol and with other of LI's structure building protocols.

Time Required for Lifespan Integration

Clients under the age of 40 can often complete one session of Lifespan Integration therapy within one hour. For older clients, clients whose early needs were not met, and clients who are very dissociated, allow 1.5 hours for each session.

When Parts of Self Interfere with LI Processing

For our purposes, a 'Part' is a neural system in and of itself. A Part exists within the self system as a separated neural network. The

Part 'sees' itself as having an existence separate from the self system, and it often acts independently and ego-dystonically. Parts can be any age and can be male or female, regardless of the client's gender. Parts can also take non-human shapes and forms. These parts of the Self were originally created by the child to help the child survive overwhelming circumstances. Children who experience trauma and neglect, without sufficient parental support to help them make sense of it, often develop part-selves or imaginary friends to help them. If these helper parts are not integrated during the course of development, they take on a life of their own which later can interfere with the functioning of the self system.

Sometimes, during the LI standard protocol, a Part will make itself known by its attempts to disrupt the process of integration. Distorted images, cartoon-like images, and non-human forms entering the imagery are all indicators of a Part at work. Clients whose bodies jerk involuntarily during state shifts when going through the Time Line often have split-off Parts existing within their self systems.

When using the Lifespan Integration standard protocol, if the adult self doesn't like the child self, the problem may be that the 'adult self' is actually not the core self, but rather is a Part. If the client expresses dislike for her child self, the therapist can finish the session by having the client imaginally bring the therapist into the imagery to care for the client's traumatized child self. The therapist should continue repetitions until the targeted source memory is clear. Any client who does not like her child self is not ready for LI standard protocol.

Clients with fragmented self systems will need to begin with the LI Attunement protocol and other structure building protocols. Repetitions of the Lifespan Integration Attunement protocol, when administered by an experienced and coherent LI therapist, will help fragmented clients to build self structure and to establish more solid connections to their core selves. When a client's self system is fragmented, a core self must be built, or the existing core must be strengthened before Parts can be successfully integrated. Often in the process of strengthening the core self, Parts are automatically integrated into the self system and are no longer problematic.

The Lifespan Integration protocol is outlined below. This is only an outline, and is not intended to be a guide for therapists using this method. LI is an extremely powerful and effective therapy. Any therapist wishing to utilize this method should attend an approved Lifespan Integration training and follow up with supervision from an approved LI consultant. An inexperienced and untrained therapist attempting this method may activate a client's material without fully integrating it. Doing LI only partly right may not help the client, and could possibly harm him.

Lifespan Integration Standard Protocol

Note: *Steps 1 and 2 are done only once, at the beginning of the session. All repetitions begin with Step 3.*

Step 1
Use an affect bridge to find the source memory which is most connected to the presenting problem.

Ask the client to focus on bodily sensations when discussing the presenting problem (or when visualizing or 'hearing' an auditory memory of a triggering incident).

Ask the client to close eyes, to let her/his mind be empty, and to tell you when a memory spontaneously surfaces.

After two or three tries, if no memory surfaces, have client choose a memory where he felt the same way he feels now re: the presenting issue. This may not resolve rhe client's presenting problem, but should resolve the chosen memory.

Step 2
Discuss the 'Source Memory'

Ask the client to tell you about the memory which spontaneously surfaced or Ask the client to tell you about the unresolved past memory which was chosen.

Step 3
Client regresses to age of child self in memory scene and points to where he feels bodily sensations. Client's current self enters memory scene to help child self.

Ask the client to go back into the source memory – to again be the child in the past scene.

Ask the client to point to where in the body he feels sensations.

Instruct the client to imagine his adult self entering the memory scene. Ask the client to tell you when the adult self is there.

When the client indicates that he has brought his adult self into the scene, the therapist says: "Tell your child self that you are his grown up self and you have come back in time to help him."

Step 4
Take the Child Self to a Peaceful Place

Ask the client to imagine taking his child self away from the memory scene and to a peaceful place. The place can be anywhere in the world. The place should be a place where the child can relax, and where the child and the adult can comfortably converse. The place can be an imagined place. It should be in past time or out of time (i.e. not in present time).

Step 5
Bring the Current Information to the Child Self

In the peaceful place, the therapist prompts the client to:
1) imaginally attend to the child's needs, and
2) tell the younger self:

"_____ happened a long time ago and it is over now."

The therapist coaches the client, giving the client words to say to his child self. The information should be brief and to the point. The therapist may also coach interactions. The therapist determines what the traumatized child needs, and what he needs to hear.

Keep statements brief and use age appropriate language. This step should take only one or two minutes maximum.

The client relays this information to his child self silently and internally.

Important: The therapist never talks directly to the client's child self. The conversation is fed from the therapist through the adult client to the client's child self.

Step 6
The Time Line of chronological images and memories

The client tells his child self that he will show him how he has grown.

The therapist reads the memory cues to the client beginning with the cue just after the source memory.

The therapist asks the client to nod after each memory. The therapists stays attuned to the client. After each nod, the therapist reads the next cue. If the client begins to flood, the therapist stays attuned and continues through the cues making sure the client is tracking.

Step 7
Bring the Child Self into the Present

When the client reaches the memory image for the current age, in present time, the therapist instructs the client to imagine bringing his child self into the home where the adult client lives now.

The therapist instructs the client to introduce his child self to family members and to repeat some of the key points, for example:

"Tell him he is safe, [the traumatic event] is over, the child is important to the adult self, etc. Be brief, and use the most applicable statements.

The therapist instructs the client to ask his child self if he has any questions.

The adult client answers the child's questions, with help from the therapist if needed.

END OF REPETITION
Take a short break. During the break the therapist asks:

If any new memories are surfacing.
If the pace through the Time Line is OK, or too fast, or too slow.
How the child self seems. What was the child's question (if any)?
Is the child responsive? attentive? distracted? depressed? anxious? excited to see the adult self?, wary of the adult self?, etc.

After the break return to **Step 3**. Repeat **Steps 3** through **7** with very short breaks between repetitions.

Continue with repetitions of **Steps 3** through **7** until the following three conditions have been met:

1) The child self has a solid understanding that he is now a part of the grown up self,
2) The child self has no further questions or concerns about the past, and
3) The client reports that a significant proportion of positive memories and images spontaneously surfaced during the last repetition of the Time Line.

On the last repetition of **Steps 3** through **7**, after the child self is in present time in the home where the client lives now, if the child has no further questions, the therapist gives the client a moment to say anything else he would like to say to the child self.

The therapist then instructs the adult client to allow the younger self to merge into the adult. This merging is symbolic and is not required.

Step 8
Check the source memory

The therapist asks the client to again view the memory scene and to be aware of the sensations he feels in his body when viewing the scene.

If integration is complete, the sensations in the client's body will be calm or neutral, and the child will be acting in a normal and age appropriate way in the image, or the child will no longer be in the image.

If the client reports that he still feels some distress in his body when he returns to the source memory, return to **Step 3** and repeat **Steps 3** thru **7**.

Continue to repeat **Steps 3** through **7** until the client is able to view the source memory scene without feeling any distress in his body.

If client's body is clear in **Step 8**, proceed to **Step 9**

Step 9
Check the Presenting Problem

Note: Skip Step 9 if the client chose the memory used in Step 1

Usually the presenting problem feels more resolved or is no longer viewed as a problem. The session is considered complete when the source memory is resolved, even if the client's presenting problem is not completely resolved.

There may be other source memories associated with the presenting problem which can be addressed and resolved in future LI sessions. Sometimes the presenting problem will be completely resolved within the first LI session, and sometimes more LI sessions will be necessary.

Important Notes:

Finish integrating the source memory before getting into a discussion with the client about any other memories.

Do not switch source memories midway through the session.

Talking about memories activates neural networks. Do not allow the client to discuss memories which come up along the Time Line unless you are certain you have enough time left in the session to process and integrate these memories.

Make a note of what other traumatic memories come up. These can be processed during a future session if the client wishes.

When Lifespan Integration therapy is done correctly, with enough repetitions of the Time Line, there is no need to contain unprocessed material at the end of the session.

Remember that integration is the key to success with LI. The LI Time Line is the integrating factor. Healing will be complete and successful if sufficient repetitions of the Time Line occur during the session.

Chapter Five
LI Protocols for Strengthening Self-Structure

There are two basic categories of Lifespan Integration protocols: 1) The trauma clearing protocols, and 2) The structure building protocols. So far in this book the focus has been on the trauma clearing protocols. This chapter looks at some of the impacts which early trauma and neglect have on a developing child, and at how this early damage can be healed using Lifespan Integration. It is beyond the scope of this book to go into detailed descriptions of the various LI structure building protocols and how each is specifically used. Mental health professionals can learn how to use these advanced techniques at the Level 2 and Level 3 Lifespan Integration trainings.

Effects of Trauma and Neglect on a Developing Child

When infants and small children experience early trauma and neglect without mediating factors, they are unable to integrate segments of their experience. When trauma and neglect occur early in life, the 'memory' of the trauma will be implicitly held in the child's body-mind. Implicit memory is emotional and somato-sensory memory. It is different from explicit memory in that it is not associated with a remembered event, and is not placed chronologically in time. Individuals who hold implicit memory of early trauma in their body-minds can easily become activated without knowing why. Survivors of childhood abuse and neglect often avoid certain activities and behaviors, hoping to prevent their implicit trauma memories from being activated.

Infants and young children are not capable of managing their emotional states. An attuned parent uses her own neurobiological system to regulate her developing child's emotional states from the beginning of the child's life and continuing until the child has internalized the ability to self-regulate.

"The mother's external regulation of the infant's developing yet still immature emotional systems during particular critical periods may represent the essential factor that influences the experience-dependent growth of brain areas prospectively involved in self-regulation." (Schore, 1994, pp. 31-32)

Unfortunately, not all parents are capable of regulating their own emotional states. Parents who can't calm themselves are also incapable of calming a distraught infant. In normal human development, infants learn to regulate emotion within the caretaker-infant dyad. If the caretaker is unable to assist the infant in this task, the infant may grow to adulthood without ever developing mechanisms for regulating and managing emotional states. As adults, these individuals will continue to have difficulties regulating their emotions and calming themselves.

Many individuals who are incapable of emotion regulation turn to external substances such as alcohol, drugs, and food, or to behaviors such as shopping, gambling, or acting out sexually. They use these substances or behaviors to regulate their emotions, often with damaging and even life threatening side effects or consequences.

LI is used to repair attachment and improve affect regulation

Secure attachment in humans is engendered through an interactive process between parent and child. Attuned states of mind between the parent and the developing child are key to the child's later ability to form attachments and to regulate emotions. A securely attached parent is able to meet the early attachment needs of his or her infant. An infant who is loved and cared for will understand at a deep level that he is important, lovable and valuable. He will grow up to be a securely attached adult. Parents who are insecurely attached will unintentionally pass their insecure attachment styles on to their children.

A child who experiences early trauma and neglect often fails to integrate a solid core self during the 'window' of early development when this integration typically occurs. When young children are mistreated or passed from one caregiver to another (as within the foster care system), they are unable to form a whole and congruent self system. These children will grow up to become adults with preoccupied, dismissive or fearful attachment styles. Lifespan Integration therapists, through repetitions of the LI Attunement protocol, are able to give these adults a second chance to develop a solid self and a secure attachment style.

"The attunement of states of mind is the fundamental way in which the brain activity of one person directly influences that of the other. Collaborative communication allows minds to "connect" with each other. During childhood, such human connections allow for the creation of brain connections that are vital for the development of a child's capacity for self-regulation". (Siegel, 2012, p. 94)

Regularly repeated sessions of the Lifespan Integration Attunement protocol will strengthen the core self of the client and bring more coherence to the client's self-system. This happens through a process which is very similar to the process of neural integration which occurs in young children during normal development.

"Attunement between child and parent, or between patient and therapist, involves the intermittent alignment of states of mind. As two individuals' states are brought into alignment, a form of what we can call "mental state resonance" can occur, in which each person's state influences and is influenced by that of the other". (Siegel, 2012, p. 95)

Following the strengthening of the client's core self, therapists are able to repair ruptures in attachment which may have occurred at various stages of development. A Lifespan Integration therapist who is attuned to his or her clients can use the structure building and affect regulating LI protocols to repair early attachment deficits. Similarly to how an attuned parent participates in the co-creation of vital neural connections and firing patterns in a developing infant or young child, therapists who are themselves coherent and securely attached can use the structure building LI protocols to attune to their clients while imaginally 'holding' them. In this way the therapist is able to 'hold' the client within his window of tolerance while leading him through the memory cues of his entire life. The feeling states existing throughout the session are felt by both client and therapist. The client feels 'held' or 'contained' while he re-experiences events from his life, including traumatic events. Through 'viewing' repetitions of his life story and concurrently feeling tolerable levels of emotion, the client is able to re-process how memory is held within his system. The feeling states associated with the re-experienced memories are integrated into the client's existing neurobiological system during each repetition of the LI time line.

Integration through the LI Time Line

Young children begin by viewing themselves as many different selves, each self being matched to a different emotional state or to a specific experience. Through the co-construction of his autobiographical narrative, a young child gradually begins to see himself as one unified self. This unified self encompasses all of his remembered experiences and emotional states up through his current age.

"Co-constructed narratives in an emotionally supportive environment can provide the necessary matrix for the psychological and neurobiological integration required to avoid dissociative reactions." (Cozolino, 2002, p. 264).

After many sessions of the LI structure building protocols, clients who began LI therapy with memory gaps are eventually able to connect the pieces of their lives into a coherent whole.

Coherent and experienced therapists get best results

The effectiveness of the LI structure building protocols is directly correlated with the knowledge, experience, skill, and coherence of the administering therapist. To effectively repair early damage and build a solid core in the client, LI requires a therapist who is able to maintain a profound attunement with the client throughout the entire LI session. Thus the quality and success of any LI work will be in direct proportion to how much work the therapist has done to heal herself through her own relationships, through her own psychotherapy, and through following a path or discipline which improves and deepens body-mind coherence.

Most people have had the experience of feeling a very peaceful energy when in the presence of an energetically coherent, grounded, loving, and open person. When one feels this peace and harmony in the presence of a spiritual Master, for example, one is feeling the harmony and coherence of his or her energy field. For best results with the Lifespan Integration structure building protocols, the therapist should be grounded, coherent, open, and loving. When attuning to a client during LI, the therapist enters a deep, peaceful, loving, and open, state. The therapist remains in this state throughout the session, and goes deeper into this state as the session progresses. During a Lifespan Integration session the energetic field between the client and therapist should replicate the ideal energetic connection between a new-born and his parents or primary caregivers. The therapist essentially 're-parents' the new-born self within the client through the "mental state resonance" established when the therapist attunes to the client. The client and therapist both benefit from the therapist's ability to enter a deep, coherent, peaceful, loving, state. In any attuned relationship both parties benefit.

A well-integrated self system is coherent. Securely attached people tell the most coherent life narratives. People who lack coherence tend to be unaware that anything is missing. As these people become more coherent, they can feel the difference in themselves by comparing to a previous, less coherent state.

While engaged emotionally with a coherent and attuned therapist, clients essentially 'download' the therapist's ability to self-regulate. In this way clients 'learn' new neural firing patterns and new ways to self-regulate. Through repetitions of their time line (life story) in the presence of an attuned therapist, their self systems become more coherent over time. This is reflected in improvements in their ability to form secure attachments and to regulate their emotions. After LI therapy, people find themselves spontaneously reacting to current stressors in more age appropriate ways. They typically feel better about their lives, their work, their relationships, and themselves.

Chapter Six
Use of Imagery and Active Imagination

It is beyond the scope of this book to describe the multitude of ways in which imagery and active imagination can be used therapeutically. Therapists who have not used imagery in their work prior to use of Lifespan Integration can still get good results with LI, but will not have as much range or versatility. Becoming more fluent in the use of imagery as a therapeutic language will allow the therapist more freedom to improvise during Steps 5 and 7 of the Lifespan Integration protocol.

An excellent outline of the basic steps of active imagination can be found in Robert A. Johnson's book: Inner Work: Using Dreams and Active Imagination for Personal Growth. For a more thorough exploration of the technique of active imagination as developed by C.G. Jung, read Barbara Hannah's Encounters with the Soul. The Jungians use active imagination for entering into dialogue with various archetypes or parts of self which reside in the unconscious. Jung used active imagination on himself, and later recommended it to many of his patients as a way to connect with unconscious aspects of the Self. However, Jung's approach didn't involve the therapist in the patient's process.

During Lifespan Integration therapy, active imagination is used to bring information and support to the child self in the memory scene. The client imaginally finds his child self in past time where he may be frozen in the past trauma. The LI therapist doesn't guide the imagery, but rather asks the client what is happening in his imagery. The therapist then directs and coaches the client with suggestions of ways to respond to what the client reports 'seeing' internally. The therapist suggests possible ways for the client to interact with his child self, and she tells the client what to say to his child self during the internal conversation. The therapist never uses 'guided imagery' as this would interfere with the client's unconscious process. In LI therapy, the imagery is generated by the client's unconscious mind. The client's image making process often offers symbolic information in the same way that dreams inform us through symbols.

Following are some general guidelines for using active imagination during Lifespan Integration therapy:

- In active imagination the individual engages interactively with his own unconscious contents.

- The therapist suggests or guides in a way that allows the client's inner material to present itself.

- The therapist asks the client what is happening in the imagery, how the child self seems, what he is doing, etc.

- The therapist uses her therapeutic skills and her knowledge of children to determine what interventions will help the child in the trauma scene.

- The therapist then coaches the adult client, telling the client what to say to his child self, using words that a child of that age will understand.

- The therapist also coaches the adult client regarding his behavior toward his child self: how to protect him, defend him, comfort him, etc.

In Lifespan Integration, imagery is used to re-visit the past to work with child selves which are stuck there. These child selves do not have the broader vision of the total self system available to them. Because they are locked into a childhood time frame, they are not always aware of the changes that have occurred over time. In Lifespan Integration therapy, the therapist coaches the client to bring the information to the child in the past. During the LI session, the adult client is regressed to being the child self. He is able to repeat the suggested statements to his child self, but he is not fully present in his adult self, and therefore is not able to think about what the child needs. In a sense, during the LI session, the adult client is a child again. He appreciates having a competent adult (the therapist) who can take charge and do what is needed to help him. This was missing at the time of the original trauma.

When using active imagination, both memories and images will present themselves, and will often be entwined. The imagery is symbolic and can be interpreted in the same way dreams can be interpreted. Often the imagery that presents itself will give the client and therapist insights which they might be unable to get through talking. A good example of this was the image of a totem pole which came to a D.I.D. client during a Lifespan Integration session. The client had been struggling for some time to understand the concept that all of her alters shared the same body and mind. She could grasp this intellectually, but on a deeper level she could not accept it. When her own body-mind system presented her with the image of the totem pole, she was at first confused. When describing this image she realized and understood that all of the beings on the totem pole were carved from the same block of wood, just as all of her alters shared the same body. This spontaneously generated image helped her to understand that she truly **was** one body-mind.

When working with child states who are frozen in past time, active imagination can be used to convey safety, support, and caring. Words telling an infant or very young child that he is safe now have no meaning. Through active imagination the adult client (as coached by the therapist) creates the conditions of safety, attachment, and attunement which will be felt by the very young child self.

Coaching Internal Conversations

Lifespan Integration utilizes a coached internal conversation between the adult client and his child ego state as a vehicle to bring current information and perspective to the child in the past. The rationale behind this approach is explained in Chapter 3, *Applied Neuroscience*. The therapist plays a very active role in this conversation, acting as a bridge between the adult client and his split off child self. During the breaks the therapist consults with the adult client to find out what was missing at the time of the trauma, and what the adult would like the child to understand from his current perspective. Later on in the protocol, the therapist puts this information into words which the child can understand, and feeds this information to the child through the adult client. As with therapy in general, it is important to respect the client's beliefs and values when coaching the internal conversation. This should not present a problem as long as the therapist coaches the internal conversation in a way which brings in only the information and support which the child self needs to resolve the past trauma.

Sometimes the client's child self needs more than current information in order to let go of the past. The therapist asks for feedback from the adult client about the child's response to the new information. Does the child believe the information? Does the child have any questions? Think of the coached internal dialogue between the client and his child self as the means to provide the child self with the therapeutic interventions that could have helped him at the time of the trauma if adequate support had been available then. These same interventions will help the child in the adult now, no matter how many years have passed, because the child state has not had access to the resources of the adult client. When working with the child in the adult, the therapist will get good results only if she uses age appropriate interventions and age appropriate language. Therapists using Lifespan Integration will get better results if they have a good rapport with children, and understand the basics of child development.

Constructed 'Memories'

When clients report limited memories of their childhoods, but have factual information from reliable sources, the therapist can use 'constructed memories'. This term is used to avoid confusion and the possible problems associated with "false memory syndrome." If facts about the early history are known and verifiable, actual memory is not necessary. A constructed memory is simply a framework. Stick to known facts.

For example: Client X grew up in a violent family. The factual information which X has reported is that his stepfather beat his mother up on several occasions beginning when X was three years old, and continuing until his mother divorced his stepfather when X was eight years old. X has been told by his mother that he witnessed most of these fights, and even tried to stop his stepfather. X has no memory of the violence, but these historical facts have been confirmed by X's grandmother, his cousins, and his older siblings. X is having problems with intimate relationships and believes his early history is part of the problem.

The early trauma can be targeted using Lifespan Integration even without an actual memory:

1) Ask X to imagine himself as a three-year-old watching his stepfather hitting his mother.

2) Ask X to be in touch with what he feels in his body as he watches this constructed memory.

3) Use the Lifespan Integration protocol to target this 'memory' beginning with Step 3.

In the example used above, X witnessed violence over a five-year period. Integrating the implicit memory from when X was three years old, as described above, will not necessarily integrate other implicit memories the client may be holding from witnessing violence at different ages and stages of development. To ensure that all the implicit memories from this time period are integrated, the therapist should target, during separate LI sessions, separate constructed memories where X 'sees' himself at various ages between age three and age eight (perhaps at 3, at 4, at 6, and at 8).

If a client has sensations in his body when imagining a 'constructed memory' scene, then he is most likely connecting to his implicit (body) memory of a similar event from his childhood. The Lifespan Integration protocol connects the child state and associated body memories to the current self of the client and to the therapist. The protocol brings energy and information to the child self, freeing him from where he has been frozen in the past memory. After sufficient repetitions of Steps 3 through 7 of the LI standard protocol, actual memories may begin to surface; however, it is not necessary for the client to ever actually remember what he experienced or witnessed as a child.

The Internal Conference Room
The internal conference room is an imaginal technique which can be used to access a client's unconscious contents. It is not advisable to use the internal conference room technique with clients who lack solid core selves. Therapists who use the conference room to 'go fishing' for fragmented parts of self run the risk of activating a

client's polarized parts. These angry and protective parts, once activated, may remain active for up to a week after the LI session, often creating havoc in the client's self-system. Most clients who have 'loose' parts lack a coherent self system. These clients will benefit most from many sessions of the Lifespan Integration Attunement protocol and other structure building protocols.

Internal Conference Room Technique:

1) Ask the client to imagine nine stairs beginning at ground level and descending below ground to a door. Tell him that on the other side of the door he will find a conference room where parts of himself can meet to converse and to work out inner conflicts. Instruct the client to close his eyes and relax, and to imagine that he is descending these stairs as he hears the count down from 9 to 1.

2) Count backwards from 9 to 1, timing each number to coincide with the client's exhaled breath.

3) When finished counting say: "Now you are at the bottom of the stairs, and when you are ready you can open the door in front of you which leads into your internal conference room." Ask the client to enter the conference room and to ask to speak to the part of himself who is responsible for the issue which is being worked on.

4) The client indicates that he has located the part. Discuss with the client what he notices about the part.

Once the chosen part is located, the adult client, as coached by the therapist, carries on an internal conversation with the part, re-negotiates the part's role in the self system, and then proves to the part that time has passed by going through Steps 6 and 7 of the Lifespan Integration protocol. In Step 6, begin the Time Line at the age the client was when the part developed its role in the self system. The part is thus able to see (through the memory images) that the conditions which were present when the part was developed have changed.

The part sees that there are more choices now, and that different roles are available for the part which could be more helpful for the self system, and more fun for the part. Being assigned a new role or 'job' helps the part to feel valued by the self system. Simply asking a part to quit the old problematic behavior will often not succeed because the old behavior is the only 'life' the part has had. Parts often fear that giving up their former role means death. Assigning the part a new role is a way to re-direct the part's behavior. The new role can simply be to play or to sing and dance more. If the part being integrated is a three-years-old part, then the new role should be a role which could be performed by a three-years-old child.

Often a part is quite relieved to see what has happened with the passage of time. When he realizes he is safe and doesn't have to be constantly vigilant, he may report that he is exhausted from working for years to protect the child self. He may feel too exhausted to think about taking on a new role. If this is the case, coach the client to find a real or imaginary resting place in present time where the part can relax and sleep.

In Step 7 of the Lifespan Integration protocol, the adult client, again coached by the therapist, reviews with the part the previously negotiated change of role. The therapist coaches the client to ask the part if he can agree to give up the old (problematic) role and replace it with the new agreed upon role. The therapist coaches the adult client to explain to the part that he now lives in present time as part of the self.

Steps 5, 6 and 7 of this modified LI standard protocol can be repeated 4 or more times. At the end of the last repetition the part can merge if desired. Successful merging is not an indication of integration. If the client does not have a solid core self, this imaginal work may appear to be successful but generally will not hold.

Chapter Seven
Treatment of Eating Disorders

Working with Anorexics

Anorexia usually develops during adolescence. Anorexics are extremely resistant to maintaining a normal, healthy body weight. They feel successful when they are able to lose weight, even if their weight is already dangerously low. Anorexics often spend an inordinate amount of time thinking about food and planning what to eat. They often have rigid controls and rituals around their food intake. They use their rituals to regulate what they will eat, and how and when they will eat it. Many anorexics engage in excessive and compulsive exercise as well. In spite of all evidence to the contrary, most anorexics do not believe that they have a problem. They feel they know better than and are superior to those who want to help them. They feel challenged to show that they have more will power and control over themselves than other people, and this seems to give them a sense of accomplishment.

I have found that with the handful of anorexics I have worked with, the ego state in charge of the client's relationship to food has been a young adolescent. This adolescent Part has hijacked or taken over operation of the self system. The anorexic Part or ego state is entrenched or 'stuck' in the past with the belief that the body is too big or too fat. Looking in the mirror doesn't help since the anorexic 'Part' sees the past body image in place of the underweight current image.

Lifespan Integration therapy can help the anorexic client to integrate the part of self who has taken over the regulation of food intake. The method below shows how LI is used to 'show' the stuck anorexic Part how time has passed and the body has truly changed. The 'Part' of the self-system in charge of the anorexic behavior is truly shocked and surprised to see the change in body size. In young anorexics who were stable and fairly 'normal' prior to the onset of the anorexia, I have seen a full and almost miraculous recovery after one or two sessions of Lifespan Integration focused on integrating the anorexic Part. If the anorexia is caught early, there is a much better chance of full recovery. If the anorexic behavior has been present and reinforced for many years, treatment with LI may or may not be helpful. For anorexics with histories of early trauma or neglect, use the Attunement protocol to establish a solid core self before attempting to integrate the anorexic ego state.

To be successful working with adolescent ego states, it is important to recognize that they are not interested in listening to adults. Giving them information and choices, and negotiating with them in a respectful manner works well.

Treatment Method Used

Explain to the client:

- There is a part of her who is trying to be helpful and make her look good, be perfect, be popular, etc.

- That part has become too powerful and is now overwhelming the system.

- This creates a problem for some of the other parts of her self system since her whole life has now become oriented around food or avoidance of food.

- Most people create parts of themselves to tackle various problems; however the self system works more efficiently when all the parts can work together as a team.

Then ask the client if she would be willing to go inside herself and have a conversation with the part in charge of her relationship with food. Make sure the client agrees on the goal, i.e. what outcome she would like. Usually the client does not want to gain weight. The goal might be to become more self-accepting, or to be less worried and obsessed about food, body fat, looking perfect, or being perfect. It is important to agree on a concrete behavioral goal before proceeding.

The therapist counts down from 9 to 1 and asks the client to close her eyes and imagine that she is walking down stairs which start at ground level. The therapist asks the client to go through the door that is at the bottom of the stairs and to find the part of herself who is in charge of food and not eating. The client lets the therapist know when she has located this part. (See previous chapter for instructions about how to use the internal conference room technique).

When the client indicates that she has found the anorexic part, instruct her to find or to create a comfortable place where the two of them can talk together. When the client is ready, begin to coach the internal conversation between the client and the ego state who is responsible for the anorexia.

1) Ask the client to introduce herself to the anorexic part of self and to tell the anorexic part that she appreciates the work the part has been doing to help her lose weight and look good.

2) Ask the client to tell the anorexic part that she has been doing such a good job that it is causing some problems. (and name possible consequences that apply such as perhaps not wanting to be required to drop out of school or to be hospitalized if more weight is lost.)

3) Ask the client how old the part is. Usually this is quite clear to the client as the younger self looks exactly as the client looked at the time of onset of anorexia – same hair style, same clothes, etc. Usually the anorexic 'Part' is a chubby adolescent – about 12 or 13 years old.

4) Instruct the client to explain to the anorexic part that many changes have occurred in her life and lots of time has gone by since the part began doing her 'job'. Ask the client to explain to the part that there are other ways that the part could be more helpful now, in the present.

5) Ask the client to explain to the anorexic part that she has grown up now and is a very important part of the grown up self, and lives with her in the present. Instruct the client to tell the part that she will show her with pictures how this has happened (how she grew up to become the older self).

6) Lead the client through the Time Line (Lifespan Integration protocol Step 6). For the first image of the Time Line, ask the client to pick a memory from shortly after the onset of the anorexia. Then proceed through the

Time Line season by season to the present. Use a memory cue list with a memory cue for each season since the onset of the anorexic behavior.

7) In Step 7 of the protocol, after the client has brought the anorexic part into the present, instruct the client to begin negotiating with the part as to what new role she would like to play (what new job she would like to have for the system). Surprisingly, food related jobs are OK. The job could be planning healthy, well-balanced meals.

8) Allow the client to take a short break. After the break:

9) Ask the client to return to the conference room and to re-enter into conversation with the anorexic part. Have the client continue the process of negotiating the new role the part will play for the self system. Ask the client to get suggestions from the part about what she might like to do other than withholding food. Repeat Step 6, the LI Time Line, proving again to the younger part-self that she is no longer a chubby adolescent, and continue with Step 7.

10) After the new role has been negotiated, have the client ask the part if she has any concerns about: 1) giving up the old role of withholding food from the system, and 2) taking on the new role. After each session of negotiation, repeat Step 6, the Time Line, and go to Step 7 bringing the younger part of self into the present life.

Concerns are often about getting fat. This can be solved by coaching the client to give the anorexic ego state factual information about what happens during the process of digestion. Coordinating with a nutritionist who will provide that factual information can also be helpful. Many anorexic ego states believe that any fat they eat will go directly through their body and deposit itself as fat somewhere where they don't want it. Anorexic ego states often carry irrational beliefs about the relationship between food intake and weight gain.

Usually the anorexic 'Part' will agree to try a new role for at least a week. It is important to let the anorexic ego state be in charge of this decision. Most ego states want to be helpful to the self system. They often have misguided ideas about what behaviors are helpful.

11) Ask the anorexic client to again thank the anorexic Part for working with her, and to tell her she will show her again the pictures of scenes from her life which will prove to her how things have changed over the past ___years since the onset of the anorexia. Lead the client through the Time Line again, season by season.

12) In Step 7, in the present, instruct the client to again go over the agreement with the anorexic Part. Coach the client to explain to the anorexic Part that time has passed, she is older now, and she is an important part of the client.

13) The internal conversation in the conference room, the journey through time, and going over the role change can be repeated again if time allows.

14) At the end of the last repetition, coach the client to ask the anorexic Part if she would like to merge her body into the client's body because she is an important part of the client. It is not necessary for the part to merge if she is not ready.

At the follow up appointment, ask the client to return to the internal conference room and to find the anorexic part. Ask the client to thank the formerly anorexic part for performing the new role in the self system. Have the client ask the formerly anorexic part if she is willing to continue performing the new role in place of the anorexic role. Help the client to resolve with the part any concerns that the formerly anorexic part may have. The client and the part may want to re-negotiate a new role for the part. After an agreement is reached between the client and the formerly anorexic part, lead the client through the Time Line, season by season, to the present. Ask the client to bring the formerly anorexic part into her present home and to go over the agreement with the part once more. The Time Line can be repeated again, season by season, while the part is with the client in her current home. At the end of the last repetition, instruct the client to tell the formerly anorexic part that time has passed and she is older now and is an important part of the grown up self. Have the client ask the formerly anorexic part if she would like to merge her body into the client's body since they are one and the same. The merging is optional.

All of the above internal conversation is between the client and the client's anorexic ego state. The client is coached by the therapist regarding what to say throughout the process. The client reports to the therapist the details of what she is hearing internally during the conversation with the anorexic ego state and the details of the ego state's behavior. Based on this feedback, the therapist determines what to have the adult client say to, or ask of the younger ego state.

Working with Bulimics and Binge Eaters

Bulimia is characterized by recurrent episodes of binge eating, and a lack of control over eating during the episode. To compensate for the binging, and to prevent weight gain, bulimics participate in some form of purging, often self-induced vomiting or misuse of laxatives. Excessive exercising may also be part of the picture. Bulimics often have a very low opinion of themselves, and are ashamed of their binging and purging. Bulimia can also be used to act out shame.

Many bulimics and binge eaters report a pattern of learning to use food for comfort at an early age. Many use binging on food to escape unpleasant mood states and to regulate emotion in the same way alcoholics use alcohol. Unlike alcoholics, who can learn to stay away from alcohol, bingers need to continue to eat food, and therefore have to learn to regulate intake. Bingers tend to have problems with limits, and often have trouble setting limits for themselves in other areas as well. They may report problems with spending, with drugs or alcohol, or with sexual promiscuity. Many of these excessive behaviors are attempts to self-soothe or to regulate affect. For these clients, finding a way to calm themselves with something other than food is crucial to the success of the work.

Beginning immediately after birth, humans use eating in the form of sucking for comfort. Affect regulation is 'learned' in the mother-infant dyad. Mothers who are unable to regulate their own emotions are not able to pass affect regulation skills on to their children. For some infants, sucking becomes important as a 'tool' used to self-soothe. When addressing problems which arise from use of food for self-soothing the therapist will need to use the LI Attunement protocol to 're-parent' the infant self within the adult client. The therapist must hold the doll representing the client's baby self, and attend to the 'baby' while remaining calm and staying attuned to the adult client. The LI Attunement protocol can also help clients who want to give up other oral fixations such as thumb sucking or smoking cigarettes, pipes, or cigars.

When using Lifespan Integration for binge eaters and bulimics, many sessions of the LI Attunement protocol may be needed. In order to reinforce the new neurological patterns for self-soothing, it is best to do these Attunement sessions weekly, or at a minimum every two weeks. With binge eaters and bulimics, the primary goal of Lifespan Integration is to improve the client's ability to regulate affect. Most binge eaters who become more skilled at affect regulation are able to give up binging and purging behaviors quite easily. Clients who have received many sessions of the LI Attunement protocol from an experienced LI therapist have reported that they are no longer able to dissociate while binging on food. Former bingers report that even when they think they want to binge, they are unable to do so. Without the ability to dissociate, clients may plan a binge, but generally will eat only a small amount and not want any more.

In most cases, it will not be necessary to address the purging behavior. When clients are able to self-soothe, and when they are no longer capable of entering the dissociative state where they would in the past have binged on food, purging is usually no longer a problem. If the client learns to self-soothe yet finds she continues to eat just so she can have the 'high' she gets from purging, then the therapist may need to use the LI Parts protocol to integrate the 'Part' who is addicted to purging.

Chapter Eight
Treatment of Dissociative Identity Disorder

In early stages of human development, the self is not unified, but rather many selves and self-states develop to respond to varying conditions and circumstances. During normal development, beginning in the second year of life, these multiple selves and self states become integrated into a coherent self system. This type of neural integration requires the co-construction of the autobiographical narrative. The child attempting to integrate experience needs to discuss the events of her life with a person or persons who are familiar with the child and with her history. Parents and other close family members are best for this role. When children experience overwhelming trauma in the absence of support and protection from adult caretakers, there is often no one with whom the child is able to discuss the traumas. In these cases there is often insufficient neural integration for the creation of a unified self. The resulting fragmented self system is often diagnosed as Dissociative Identity Disorder.

When children grow up in an environment of trauma and/or neglect, their many part-selves become specialized. Some hold traumatic memory, some hold the memory of physical pain, while others specialize in primitive defenses such as fight, flight, or freeze. When parental support is lacking, or when children are prohibited from discussing the traumatic events they have experienced, the co-construction of narratives required for neural integration does not occur. Growing up without the ability to discuss and share their life stories, these traumatized individuals remain fragmented. Their many selves and self-states remain only partially integrated. Some part-selves, also known as 'alters', are held in the neural system separately.

Lifespan Integration is extremely effective in the treatment of Dissociative Identity Disorder. LI therapy integrates the Alters or Part-selves of the D.I.D. into a unified self system. The traditional method of working with Dissociative Identity Disorder begins with delineating and mapping the separate identities of the various alters. This outmoded method now seems unnecessary and counter-productive. Given what we now know about developmental neurobiology, it seems self-evident that working separately with Alters will only strengthen their perceptions of being unique and separate from the self system.

Alters can be thought of as somewhat independent neural networks which exist outside of the core Self. Because they exist outside of the core, they are often unaware of much of the self system, and they believe themselves to be separate. When the core self is very weak there may be multitudes of these specialized neural networks (part-selves) which exist outside of the core. Repetitions of the structure building Lifespan Integration protocols will strengthen the client's core self.

Guidelines for using Lifespan Integration to treat DID and DDNOS

- Make sure the core self of the client is forward in the self system throughout the LI session. Reading cues to an alter will not bring about integration.

- Ask the client to keep her eyes open throughout the session.

- The therapist stays profoundly attuned to the client throughout the session.

- Both therapist and client must stay grounded and present (in their bodies).

- Use one of the structure building protocols: Baseline, Cell Being, or Attunement. Start with the structure building protocol which best suits the needs of the individual client.

- The therapist maintains a loving attunement with the client's infant self throughout the session.

- There is no imaginal merging at the end of the session.

- Space sessions two weeks apart. This gives the client time to return to full functioning after each session, yet reinforces the integration before too much regression occurs. Some clients may be able to tolerate weekly Attunement sessions.

- Be patient. Look for slow but steady progress. If progress is not evident, seek supervision from an approved LI consultant.

Helping the Dissociative Client to Prepare Memory Cues

Memories of dissociative clients tend to be sketchy and limited. Often there are gaps of several years. Often the memories are out of order. Before beginning Lifespan Integration work with dissociative clients, the therapist and client work together to create a written memory cue list. To prepare this cue list, the therapist and client spend a few sessions together working on a chronological list of the events from the client's life which are remembered by the client. The therapist attempts to elicit as much history as is possible from the client. Photographs of the client at various stages of her life can be helpful in constructing the memory cues if they are available; however the client must actually remember the event portrayed by the photograph. The client, if stable, may also be able to work at home between sessions on this outline of her chronological history. The list of events should start as early in the client's life as is possible, and should continue all the way to the present. The written memory cue list may end up being quite sketchy. There may be gaps of two or three years. It is not wise to begin LI with a client who has memory gaps larger than three years. Continue working with the dissociative client in other ways until a somewhat coherent memory cue list has been constructed.

Explaining the Integration Process to the D.I.D. Client

Gaining and maintaining the trust of the D.I.D. client's self system is crucial to the success of this work. It is important for the therapist to explain to the core self of the client and to whatever alters happen to be listening that the goal of integration will eventually benefit all of the alters or parts of the self system. Many parts will be threatened at first. Because alters typically develop very early in life, care must be taken to use language that can be understood by very young children. The parts of the system all need reassurance that they are valuable to the system and that no one is trying to banish or exile them. In the early stages of working with a D.I.D. individual, many of her alters will not understand much of what is being said. They will understand the words, but the words will not fit into their 'reality'.

After experiencing many sessions of the LI Attunement protocol, and after repeatedly viewing their lives as a continuous flow of selves and self-states across time and space, the part-selves or alters will begin to integrate as they 'understand' that there is a larger 'reality' than the one they have inhabited.

Using Lifespan Integration with the D.I.D. Client

The D.I.D. client who wants to work on integration using this method should understand that the work will be successful only if she is able to stay present as much as possible throughout the repetitions of the Lifespan Integration Time Line. If the client dissociates while going through the Time Line, one or more alters will enter and push the core self farther back in the self system. Without the client's core self present, the work will not succeed.

The therapist reads the Time Line memory cues, and asks the D.I.D. client to give a signal each time she has the memory image in her mind. If no signal is forthcoming after a few seconds, the therapist can call the client by name. This will bring the core self of the client forward to re-engage in the process. Dissociative clients seem better able to stay present if they keep their eyes open during all of the active imagination, and when going through time in Step 6. Repeated sessions of the Lifespan Integration Attunement protocol, spaced weekly or every two weeks, will strengthen the D.I.D. client's core self. After the core self has become "solid enough", an experienced LI therapist will be able to use the Preverbal Attachment Repair protocol to repair the attachment deficits which the client likely suffered at various stages of development.

If the D.I.D. client has trouble staying grounded and present in her body, grounding exercises may be used throughout the protocol.

1) Have the client hold something with a strong odor such as vanilla or peppermint. When the client dissociates, ask her to take a whiff of what she is holding.

2) Have the client rub her feet on the floor and her hands on the arms of her chair. Tell her to feel the ground beneath her feet and the texture of the chair upholstery.

3) Have the client say out loud: "I am (client's name)." "I am here." "I am ___ years old."

Observations

- For Lifespan Integration to be successful with D.I.D. clients, the core self must remain present, and the core self must prevent switching between alters from occurring during the LI session.

- More memories including positive (resource) memories spontaneously surface in D.I.D. clients as Lifespan Integration therapy progresses. These memories help the clients to 'connect the dots' and to fill in some of the missing pieces of their lives.

- The Time Line images are probably 'viewed' by many alters or parts simultaneously.

- In the process of creating a solid core using the LI structure building protocols, parts and alters seem to spontaneously integrate as they would have done during normal development.

Chapter Nine
Integration of Separated Self-States

Separated states of the self have been called many names over time and across models. Depending on the therapist's training and the therapeutic model used, they can be called part-selves, part objects, ego states, sub-personalities, inner children, or feeling-toned complexes to name a few. It is beyond the scope of this book to justify the existence of these 'parts' or to explain how they comprise the self system in every individual. In his excellent book, *Internal Family Systems Therapy*, (Guilford Press: 1995), Richard Schwartz clearly describes how individuals can be viewed as systems, and the methods he has developed for working with these systems. In healthy, well-adapted individuals, the internal parts work together somewhat seamlessly as a team under the competent leadership of the Self.

Many individuals who come to us as clients find that they have parts of themselves which are acting out in unhealthy and self-destructive ways. Often clients will report that they "know better" or want something different for themselves, but feel powerless against a part of themselves that seems to take over from time to time.

Using Lifespan Integration to integrate separated self states can be tricky. Therapists should not attempt this variation of LI until they have taken all three levels of Lifespan Integration training. Furthermore, therapists should not attempt to integrate separated self states in clients who lack a solid core self. As a solid core is built through many sessions of the LI structure building protocols, many previously separate parts will spontaneously integrate. After sufficient sessions of the LI Attunement protocol have brought about a more solid core and an attachment to Self, the client may notice that parts who previously 'hijacked' the self-system now remain peacefully in the background or are no longer in evidence.

Parts are threatened by integration. To them integration means their end, or their death. This is why it is important to explain to the part how much it is appreciated and how the self system needs it to play a different role. The purpose of giving the part a new job is to have the part feel valued and needed by the self system. The new 'job' should be age appropriate and something the part would like to do. Parts are usually very young despite their outward appearance. They have limited understanding and limited abilities because they are stuck in the past at the age of the client when the client created them.

Dissociative clients are often quite skilled at imagery and may appear to integrate separated self states using the internal conference room technique outlined in Chapter 6. However, if the client lacks a solid core self, this perceived 'integration' is nothing more than a mental exercise. No true integration can take place when there is no solid core Self into which the separate Part (neural network) can integrate. Working with fragments of the self system can be entertaining for both client and therapist, but in most cases work with separated fragments or parts of the self system is not effective. Most clients who present with separated self states will need many repetitions of the Lifespan Integration Attunement protocol to build a solid core self. Most clients who have a solid core Self do not have parts who act independently of the self system.

Polarized Parts

Separated self-states are often polarized or further split into sub-sets. Richard Schwartz (1995) does a thorough job of explaining polarized parts and the complexities inherent in internal systems work. Sometimes extreme aspects of parts are frightening to the clients whose systems created them. In these cases the therapist should remind the client that her child self created the part to protect herself from real or perceived dangers, and that at the core of the scary part is a frightened child self. The extremity and complexity of the internal parts which comprise the client's self system seem to reflect the extremity and complexity of the child's early environment.

Within most fragmented self systems there are polarized protective parts connected to the wounded child parts. These protective parts tend to hide out deep within the system, coming forward when they perceive a need to protect the wounded child parts. In the process of attempting to integrate a wounded child part, the associated, protective part may become activated. This may not be apparent at the end of the Lifespan Integration session, but may cause problems for the client shortly after the session and for the week following. This is another reason why it is not advisable to attempt to integrate separated Parts of the self system before there is a solid core Self. It is more effective to use the Lifespan Integration Attunement protocol consistently, every week or every two weeks. Over time this will bring about integration and coherence within the entire self system.

Integration of Somatic Memory

When a client has body pain which appears to be a somatic memory, integrating the somatic feeling state which has been holding the pain can sometimes end the physical sensation of pain. This works for neural memory of pain - when pain exists and yet there is no physical reason for the pain.

Use standard protocol Lifespan Integration and ask the client to focus on the physical pain in her body (instead of the emotions she feels in her body). Use Step 1 to find the memory associated with the somatic state. In Step 1 clients with solid core selves can usually follow an affect bridge from the felt physical pain to connect to the memory associated with the somatically remembered physical pain. When following the affect bridge back through time to find the associated pain memory, clients are often surprised that the memory which comes up is not the one the client expected.

Clients without solid cores are generally not able to successfully follow affect in their bodies. These clients can choose a memory from when they believe they first felt the physical pain which they are trying to clear. When the memory is chosen as opposed to 'found' by the affect bridge, there is less chance of successfully clearing the pain memory.

To clear the pain memory, continue with standard protocol LI. Instruct the client to imaginally bring her current self into the memory scene. The client imagines taking her child self to a peaceful place. In the peaceful place the therapist coaches the adult client to thank the child self for being brave and holding the pain for so many years. The therapist coaches the client to explain to the child self that time has passed and her body has grown and healed from the past physical injury. The therapist then leads the client through the Time Line memory cues (Step 6). Repeat the entire sequence three to five times or until the somatic pain memory has cleared.

Chapter Ten
Re-Sourcing and Re-Connecting
to Essence and to Being

Human beings contain within themselves an abundance of emotional, intellectual, and spiritual resources. For some individuals, these resources are available to them in certain areas of their lives, and yet there are parts of themselves that do not have access to these resources. A man could be an excellent parent to his children, and yet he might feel unable to parent the young, scared parts of himself. He perhaps depends on his wife to parent him, and if she leaves him he feels abandoned, frightened, alone, and incapable of caring for himself. Likewise a woman could be a very competent district attorney at her job, and yet she might allow herself to be emotionally, verbally, or even physically battered at home. These disconnects within individuals are a result of incomplete neural integration. Through correct use of Lifespan Integration therapy, clients will spontaneously connect to whichever of their own internal positive resources are relevant to their presenting problem.

Lifespan Integration also reconnects individuals to their essence and to being. In *Elements of the Real in Man* (1987), A.H. Almaas describes how, during the process of development and through interactions with the environment, a loss of essence occurs.

> When a baby is born, it is pretty much all Essence or pure Being. Its essence is not, of course, the same as the essence of a developed or realized adult. It is a baby's essence—non-differentiated, all in a big bundle. As the infant grows, the personality starts developing through interactions with the environment, especially the parents. Since most parents are identified with their personalities and not with their essence, they do not recognize or encourage the essence of the child. After a few years, Essence is forgotten, and instead of Essence, there is now personality. Essence is replaced with various identifications. The child identifies

with one or the other parent, with this or that experience, and with all kinds of notions about itself. These
identifications, experiences, and notions become con-
solidated and structured as the personality. The child
and, later, the adult believes this structure is its true
self. (pp.1-2)

Almaas goes on to describe how most adults become identified
with their personality structures, or egos, and become disconnected
from their spiritual selves, or Essence.

There is nothing bad about having a personality. You
have to have one. You couldn't survive without it. However, if you take the personality to be who you truly
are, then you are distorting reality because you are
not your personality. The personality is composed of
experiences of the past, of ideas, of notions, of identifications. You have the potential to develop a real
individuality, the Personal Essence, which is different
from the personality that covers the loss of Essence,
but this potential is usually taken over by what we call
our ego, our acquired sense of identity.

As we become more and more caught up in our lives, our relationships, and our professional duties, we become dissociated from our
true inner selves, from our Essence and Being.

Client's Description of Re-connection to Essence
Following is an extensive statement which was written for me
by a client, midway through her work with Lifespan Integration. The
client is a very gifted woman in her mid-thirties who was molest-
ed, neglected, verbally and emotionally abused, shamed, and abandoned in childhood by her parents, who were both high functioning
alcoholics. As a young adult this client was violently raped. In her
statement (below) she describes her experience going through the
LI Time Line. Her statement describes the re-connection to Essence
discussed above.

I found the visual Time Line to be very effective
and helpful in several ways, and certain aspects I find
very interesting.

78

One surprising thing that arose from this was that as I was 'bringing forward' a particular segment of myself that had enforced a negative cognition that:

"I must fail to be a success," or "I am successful only if I am failing, or a failure," that segment of myself proudly claimed responsibility for some of the lowest points of my adult life. This part of me learned that I needed to fail in order to be successful when I was around 4 or 5 years of age. The proud, confident, elated, and successful feelings I experienced as 'we' passed these low points was very powerful and really amazing.

Another interesting aspect to discover was that different traumatized segments of myself were aware of each other. One very young part of me was aware of a part of me frozen in my teens (4 or 5 years old knew about 16 years old). The younger part of me wanted to know if it had been as strong and successful in its 'duty' to protect my psyche as the teenager had been. The sincerity of the inquiry and the ferocious need to be equally adequate was very surprising. I didn't expect myself to compare myself to myself with such a competitive nature. Only after I had assured this segment of myself that it had done a wonderful job, at least as good as the teenager, was it willing to pass the teen section of my life, and come join me in being an adult.

Using the visual Time Line, joyous emotions have returned to me that I have not experienced in many years, decades even. As I learned not to trust or exuberate from the elated depths of my soul, I lost the ability to experience those emotions. Lifespan Integration has returned these emotions to me in their full Technicolor strength, but I have the adult's ability to constrain the powerful childhood emotions. The traumas stole my 'happy' palate of emotions while leaving the 'grim' one intact. 'Grim' still exists, and is slowly losing its primary place due to my experience with Lifespan Integration. Traveling through the Time Line has returned the ability to access the pure 'happy' palate again.

Also seeing myself from the very young child's perspective has really been amazing. I'm astounded by the credibility I have with my younger self. As an adult,

I've become a volunteer firefighter and am presently a professional EMT and a paramedic student. While traveling through the Time Line, I am astounded that younger traumatized parts of myself are aware of what I do for a living. (The field of paramedicine did not even exist when I was young.) How would they know an "ambulance driver" has come to take them out of there? The way these traumatized and injured child parts of me have so eagerly grasped my hand and were so willing to come with me to "where we live now" has been humbling. But also their bold, blind, belief in the firefighter or ambulance driver has strengthened me amazingly at a very deep level of belief in my own ability and confidence. That they 'see' me in my turnouts or uniform is amazing. I don't see myself that way. How do they?

Gaining the trust of several of the teenage sections of me was challenging, but also gave me access to some of the best parts of me that give and have given me my greatest strengths throughout life. Their enthusiasm at discovering that 'we' actually are living my dreams that were established in my teen years not only gives me a wonderful sense of completion I did not experience prior to doing the Time Line, but also their enthusiasm and joy are wonderful and endearing to have with me while practicing my professions. What a joy it is to have these parts of me here in the present with me. How do you miss what you never knew was lacking? But to feel the astounding fullness and completeness that having these missing segments 'returned' to me has brought about has only made me more committed to 'rounding up' the other parts still lost and frozen in time due to traumas, and 'herding' them along the Time Line and bringing them into the future together with me (us) as an integrated whole.

Spontaneous Resourcing during Lifespan Integration

Spontaneous resourcing will always occur after trauma has cleared if the therapist allows time for enough repetitions of the Time Line.

For severely traumatized individuals, six or more repetitions may be needed before resource memories begin to surface. Because of how memories are held neurologically, the memories related to perceived dangers will generally surface first. The positive resources related to the targeted issue will begin to surface and be integrated only after the 'bad' memories have emerged and have been integrated. During repetitions of the LI protocol, the client will first remember all the times in his life when he experienced difficult situations or traumas similar to the source memory. These unpleasant memories are retrieved first as a result of the defensive strategies employed in our neural programming. Correct use of Lifespan Integration requires repeating Steps 3 through 7 until resource memories spontaneously emerge.

For most clients, positive memories begin to spontaneously surface during the third repetition of the Time Line. The memories which spontaneously surface in this way will be the flip side of the earlier memories or will be new memories of times when the client prevailed in situations somehow similar to the source memory. It seems as though the psyche first offers the 'watch out for this' list of similar past experiences, and then offers the list of 'what has worked' in past situations to resolve this particular type of difficulty. With repeated 'viewings' of the events in his life related to the presenting problem, the client is able to see his strengths. Through repetitions of the LI Time Line he also gains perspective and insights about how his expectations and responses have contributed to outcomes.

Occasionally during Step 1 of standard protocol LI, when the client begins as usual with the bodily sensations related to the presenting problem, instead of landing on a traumatic memory, he arrives at a positive memory. This is an indication that the client's body-mind, in its own wisdom, has chosen to integrate past strengths which may have been forgotten or lost with the passage of time. Integrating past resource memories heals and strengthens the client, and makes it easier for the client to target and clear difficult and traumatic memories during future sessions. This happens rarely, but when it does, the therapist should continue with the protocol, adapting it as needed to integrate the positive source (resource) memory.

Case Example of Spontaneous Resourcing during LI

Bob is a 50-year-old man who reports he has been unhappily married for thirty-two years. He married his girlfriend, Kate, when she became pregnant a few months into their relationship. Bob first dated Kate when he was an 18-years-old virgin. Kate had been sexually active for several years, and had had an earlier pregnancy terminated. Kate had assured Bob that she was taking birth control pills when in fact she wasn't. Bob had been brought up in a religious tradition which values marriage and family, and does not condone divorce. Bob explained that he and Kate were from very different backgrounds, and have always had different interests. Now that their children are grown, he feels that he and Kate have nothing in common. They lead separate lives and have no emotional or sexual intimacy.

Bob's goal for therapy was to regain respect for himself. He reported feeling trapped, empty, and unhappy. He remembers a time when he liked himself and what he stood for. Bob stated he now feels alienated from himself, and has no respect for who he has become. Bob told me that he knows in his heart that his relationship with Kate is over, and that he would like to be able to tell Kate honestly how he feels, and end the marriage.

Step 1:

Bob imagined himself having a conversation with Kate, telling her honestly how he feels about her and their relationship, and telling her he wants to end the marriage. Bob was aware of what he felt in his body as he imagined this scene and conversation. Bob reported feeling a tightness across his chest and around his neck. Bob continued to focus on these bodily sensations and allowed his mind to be empty.

Source Memory:

Bob followed the affect bridge back to a memory of almost drowning in the ocean when he was 18 years old. He had broken his back in a surfboard accident, and he recalled struggling to get out of the water. In the memory he could feel his wetsuit really tight around his neck. He recalled how good he felt once he was out of the water and on the beach. Even though he was in physical pain, he was alive and had saved himself. Bob said: "I get the connection. My marriage is drowning me and I need to save my life by getting myself out of it."

Note that Step 1 of standard protocol LI was used as usual. No suggestion was made re: finding a positive, resourcing source memory. When LI is done correctly, the client's body-mind system 'decides' what memory to go back to. Going back to a resource memory is rare, but this does occur occasionally.

Steps 3 - 5:

Bob imagined being his 18-years-old self again, with his back broken, on the beach. Bob noticed the sensations in his body when he was back in time in the memory scene. Next Bob imagined his current 50-years-old self entering the memory scene on the beach. 50-years-old Bob introduced himself to young Bob, and thanked him for saving his life. Older Bob told his 18-years-old self that he could use the younger Bob's help in his present situation. Older Bob explained to his younger self that the 18-years-old Bob has grown up and is now an important part of the older Bob. Bob told his younger self that he would show him his life story and prove to him that he is now a part of the older Bob.

Step 6:

The therapist led Bob through his time line of memory cues, beginning with the cue for age 19 and ending in present time.

Step 7:

After Bob remembers the image and associated sensations for his most recent memory cue, (in present time), Bob imagines bringing 18-years-old Bob into the present, into his current home. Bob said to his younger self: "See, you are a part of me, and this is where we live now." Bob asked his 18-years-old self if he would be willing to remain in the present with the older Bob. He explained that the older Bob needs the strength and self-assuredness of the younger Bob. Bob explained to his younger self that younger Bob does not need to stay frozen in the past in the scene where he almost drowned, because he has grown up and become the adult Bob, and he lives in the present as an important part of the system that is Bob. After older Bob finished the conversation with younger Bob, he imagined his younger self merging with him—becoming one.

Step 8:

Bob remembered the near drowning experience and paid attention to what he noticed in his body. Bob reported feeling a sense of relief.

Step 9:

Bob imagined having an honest conversation with Kate. Bob reported that he felt more at ease and more ready to say what he needed to say, though he knew it would be hard to witness Kate's responses and or reactions to what he planned to say to her.

The above case demonstrates how strengths and resources can be held in younger ego states, and can be accessed and integrated through use of the Lifespan Integration protocol. Resources that are accessed and integrated in this way remain available to the whole self system.

Chapter Eleven
Specialized Uses of Lifespan Integration

Treatment of PTSD with Lifespan Integration

Post traumatic stress is a condition which results when the body 'believes' that the traumatic danger is still imminent. When a person has flashbacks and other PTSD symptoms, his body is still guarding against the possible re-occurrence of the traumatic event.

The LI PTSD protocol is very effective in proving to the client's body-mind system that the trauma is over. The LI PTSD protocol is simply an adaptation of the LI Time Line. As the body begins to understand that 'it' is no longer trapped in the traumatic situation, breathing will deepen and other signs of bodily release and relaxation will be evident. The therapist watches the client's body closely during the repetitions of the LI PTSD Time Line. The client's body shows the therapist when to move faster and when to slow down while reading the cues. The client needs to re-experience each memory scene only long enough for the related neurons to become slightly activated. In order to clear the trauma and heal, the person must touch on each aspect of the trauma. As with any LI protocol, the therapist's attunement when leading the client through the cues is necessary for a good outcome. If a client remains too long in any part of the trauma, there is the risk of too much activation leading to re-traumatization. The subsequent cue will move the client along in his internal visual 'narrative' of the trauma. It doesn't matter if the next cue is even worse, as long as the client moves there, and then continues on through the 're-play' of the trauma.

The PTSD cues go in detail through each aspect of the traumatic memory, then slowly through the days and weeks following the trauma, and then month by month to the present. If the trauma occurred several years ago, adapt the LI Time Line to go in detail through all stages of the traumatic time period, then day by day and week by week for the first month or two after, then month by month for the first year, season by season for the next year or two, and then year by year to the present. The cues can begin either immediately before the trauma (the day before a diagnosis of cancer for example, or the moment before a car wreck), or they can begin at the first moment of the trauma.

Before beginning this work, the therapist should be sure there is enough time in the session to both write the cues delineating the trauma details, and have enough remaining time in the session for several repetitions of the PTSD cues including continuing through to the present on each repetition. If the traumatic event occurred several years ago, the client's cue list for his entire life should already be completed and in the therapist's file before doing this PTSD work.

To begin, the therapist asks the client to describe what he remembers about the traumatic time period. The therapist must keep the narrative going by asking repeatedly: "And then what happened?" "And then what happened next?" Notes should be written quickly as the client continues with the narrative of the traumatic event. The therapist continues by asking what happened in the days, weeks, and months following the traumatic time period. The client's memories may be sketchy. Keep the client talking and moving through the trauma and through the weeks and months after the trauma.

Going through the details of the trauma in this way will activate the client's memory and emotions related to the trauma. Even while the PTSD cues are being written, the therapist needs to keep the client moving through time to avoid flooding. Writing the cues thus becomes the 1st repetition of the PTSD Time Line. If the trauma happened several years ago, then for each repetition the therapist reads the detailed PTSD cues covering the traumatic event and then moves directly into the regular cue list reading one cue per year from the end of the trauma all the way to the present.

It is not necessary to have a cue for each detail. Too many cues will make it impossible to get through enough repetitions. The cues should be sufficient so that the therapist can lead the client through each important scene in the 'video' of the trauma. The cues will allow the client to bring up much more detail within his mind as he repeatedly goes through the events.

With each repetition of the PTSD cues, as the client's mind brings up the images and emotions related to the trauma, more details and new memories of the traumatic time period will surface. At each short break the client can report briefly on this expansion. The therapist can add any significant new memories to the cue list, and can incorporate them during the next repetition. It is not necessary to add every new detail.

The therapist may need to read through the cues ten or more times before the client's body is convinced that the trauma is over. There is no need for any talking. This is not standard protocol. It is not necessary to bring the current (older) self into the trauma scene unless the client was a child at the time of the trauma. It is not necessary to go to the peaceful place. The PTSD protocol is like doing many repetitions of Step 6 with very short breaks in between repetitions.

The therapist reads through the cues very quickly on the first few repetitions, gradually giving more and more time between cues. On the last repetition the client should be able to watch the internal 'video' of the traumatic time period without having an emotional reaction. While reading through the trauma cues, the therapist should watch the client closely for signs of emotion. If the client becomes too activated, the therapist must move more quickly through the cues. The trauma will be completely clear when the therapist is able to read slowly through all the cues while the client stays present, watching the 'movie' of the traumatic time period, without experiencing bodily distress. Most traumas can easily be cleared within one extended LI session (1.5 hours). When the trauma is clear, the client will be able to 'watch' it from a distance even if the effects of the trauma (injuries from an accident for example) are still affecting the client.

Note: Clear only one trauma at a time, even if several different traumas occurred in sequence.

Trauma memories are encoded in the body-mind in separate networks. Some clients may have experienced many separate traumas all within a relatively short time frame. Therapists will have better results if they separate the traumas and clear them individually. It usually works best to clear the most recent traumas first. The trauma cues for the most recent trauma will bring the client from the recent trauma back to present time without going through all the previous traumas.

Note: When clearing trauma, all the needed repetitions of the PTSD cues must occur in the same session.

The most common mistake made by therapists using the PTSD protocol is using too many cues, talking too much, and getting in too few repetitions. If the therapist runs out of time before completing the optimal number of repetitions, the net effect on the client is activation of the body memory of the trauma without resolution. Repetitions of trauma cues are not cumulative from session to session.

Doing 5 repetitions of trauma cues three weeks in a row will repeatedly activate the trauma memory without fully clearing it. This will reinforce the neural networks relating to the trauma which will make it more difficult to clear. Inexperienced therapists should allow 2 or more hours to ensure enough time for adequate repetitions of the PTSD cues.

Lifespan Integration for Depression and Anxiety

Clients who present with chronic depression often experienced neglect, abandonment, or the loss of an important attachment figure during childhood. For these clients the core issues are loneliness, emptiness, and feeling unloved or unlovable. In addition, depressed clients often carry shame about the early neglect or abandonment. Chronically anxious or depressed clients may have experienced birth trauma, early neglect, or both. If the client's history indicates neglect, trauma, or significant separation from mother at any time during the client's first two years of life, the therapist should use the LI Attunement protocol, and then the attachment repair process for any applicable early stages of development.

Many depressed clients contain needy child states who are 'looking for love'. These clients often have made poor choices in relationship in an attempt to get partners to meet their early attachment needs. Relationships which are initiated in hopes of getting early needs met are destined to fail unless both partners are able to grow and mature as the relationship progresses into new stages. When insecure attachment is at the root of the client's relationship failures, the client will benefit most from many sessions of the LI Attunement protocol with the therapist holding the doll representing the client's newborn self.

If, on the other hand, the depressed or anxious client appears securely attached and her attachment history reflects this, then it is likely that she at some point suffered a significant loss in one of her primary attachment relationships. If a person who was securely attached as a child becomes depressed later in life, it is likely that a significant loss occurred in childhood after attachment had been established. A recent event in the client's life may have activated the earlier loss.

When working with depressed or anxious clients, the therapist must first determine whether the client's depression is due to loss of an attachment figure, or due to deprivation or trauma during the attachment process. Securely attached clients who are depressed can often be healed quickly using a variation of LI standard protocol.

To work with depression in cases where the early attachment needs were met, determine when the problem began. Perhaps the child was secure until the family moved to a new town and the mother went to work. In this case the therapist asks the client to choose any memory of being alone and lonely in the new town. It can be a generic memory as opposed to being a specific day which is remembered. Use this as the 'source' memory.

Have the client begin by being the child self in the memory. The client points to where she feels sensation in her body (step 3). Depressed clients are somewhat numb but should be able to feel some sensation. Coach the client to imagine her adult self coming into the memory scene to connect with her child self.

Important: At this point the therapist asks the adult client how she feels about her child self. A securely attached client will feel compassion and love for her child self. If the client is unable to feel positive feelings toward her child self, she is not ready for standard protocol LI. Instead use the LI structure building protocols to strengthen the client's core self.

For clients who feel positively toward their younger selves, continue as with standard protocol LI. In the peaceful place the therapist coaches conversations and interventions. The therapist coaches the client to say for example: "Tell your younger self that you are sorry she was alone when her mom had to be gone so much. Tell her that was a long time ago and now she is not alone because you are always with her." The therapist coaches the adult self to express and demonstrate how the adult self values the child self. The interventions should give the child self information and experiences which will reverse the interpretations resultant from the early loss of relationship with the attachment figure. The coached statements or actions are designed to fit the age of the child and to counter any shame which resulted from the breaks in early attachment.

After about one minute of coaching and giving time for the imagined interactions, the therapist leads the client through time, beginning with the memory cue just after the age of the source memory. Remember that the positive changes in the child self's feeling state, which are generated during the imagined interactions, will be integrated into the client's self-system only if there are sufficient repetitions of the Time Line. When the adult client imagines bringing the child self into her home in present time (step 7), more interaction can be coached before the break. After a short break repeat Steps 3 through 7 of the LI standard protocol, as modified above. Three to five repetitions, taking short breaks as needed at the end of each repetition, should be sufficient. After the last repetition of Steps 3 through 7, the child ego state can merge into the adult if desired.

Note: *An 'adult' self who dislikes a child ego state is not the core self but rather is a different part or fragment of the total self. The core self is whole and will love all parts of self. If the client lacks a solid core self, it is not possible to repair attachment losses or to create relationship within the self-system using standard protocol LI.*

Anxiety Due to Birth Trauma or Early Separation

Generalized anxiety is often related to birth trauma and/or to early separation from the mother. Most people who were kept in an incubator or an isolette due to premature birth will experience generalized anxiety. This level of anxiety feels 'normal' to them because they have always felt it. When working with anxious clients, the therapist should first assess for birth trauma, early separation from mother, and/or trauma or neglect during the first two years of life (before explicit memory is encoded). Clients who were adopted, even if adopted at birth, experience a separation from their biological mothers. If any of the above factors apply, then begin with the LI structure building protocols. Later the LI Birth to Present protocol can be used to clear any birth trauma, and Preverbal Attachment repair can be used to repair attachment deficits which may have occurred at various stages of development

Anxiety Due to Too Much Early Responsibility

Another type of anxiety occurs in clients who experienced neglect and/or overwhelming responsibilities when they were children. As adults, when under stress, they will revert to handling responsibilities from the same neural networks which were originally developed to cope with the stressors of childhood. When this happens they are not in touch with their full adult capabilities, and consequently they often feel overwhelmed, inadequate, and anxious. Standard protocol LI will connect the overly responsible child ego state within the adult client to the competent adult self. This will significantly reduce the level of anxiety experienced by the client even when under stress.

Ask the client to choose a memory of a time when he was overwhelmed with responsibilities as a child or teenager. Begin standard protocol LI with the client imagining his child-self alone in the chosen memory scene (step 3). The adult client imaginally enters the memory scene and takes the younger self to a peaceful place. In step 5 the therapist should coach the client to tell the younger self that the adult will handle all the responsibilities, pay the bills, etc, and the child can now play and enjoy life. The goal is to transfer the current life tasks and responsibilities over to the adult self of the client, freeing the anxious child self. The child self may at first be reluctant to trust the adult self to handle the responsibilities. Continue with repetitions and this should change as the child self begins to understand that time has passed. In the peaceful place (Step 5) and in the home in Step 7 the therapist coaches the adult client to interact with the child in ways which will help the child self to feel valued, loved, cared for, and protected. Depending on the client's history, this variation of LI can be done for several ages and stages of the client's over-burdened childhood.

Anxiety and Panic Attacks Due to Repressed Rage

Sometimes anxiety and/or panic attacks are due to an unconscious fear that underlying rage may burst through. This type of anxiety is often experienced by people who live or work in abusive situations. They may feel trapped in their situations and unable to express their normal and appropriate anger toward the person on whom they depend. When a person is dependent on an abusive parent, partner, or boss, the natural impulse to express anger must be suppressed. Keeping the rage suppressed requires enormous energy and often results in anxiety or panic attacks. Very often the current situation is related to a similar situation in the past. If the client focuses on the bodily sensations of fear or powerlessness, she may connect to a childhood memory where she felt the same fear or powerlessness. Coaching the adult client to express anger on behalf of the child self in this past memory will release anger from the client's self system and thus reduce the anxiety and end the panic attacks. Addressing past abuse and releasing anger about past events will help the client feel more empowered to address the abusive situation in the present.

Preverbal Trauma

If the client experienced trauma or neglect during his first two years of life, there will be body memory, but usually no explicit memory of what happened. Infants and very young children do not yet have enough cortical consolidation to encode explicit memories. Instead, experiences, feelings, and images are encoded in implicit memory. When implicit memories are 'remembered' the client will 'retrieve' a feeling state, and may report bodily sensation. Sometimes a client will have a sense of his very young self being alone and frightened, or of trying to get away from something big and scary. If the early abuse was physical or sexual, somatic memory will often be present and can give clues about the nature of the trauma.

If the trauma goes back to infancy, the client may describe feeling fragmented, or may report feelings which are generalized through-out his body, such as restlessness extending to his arms and legs. Clients who were born prematurely and who spent their early days in incubators describe feeling generalized anxiety throughout their bodies, and a sense of being fragmented or falling apart. One client who spent time in an incubator during infancy reported having recurring nightmares about huge 'refrigerators' with tubes and ma-chine-like robots.

Frequently when clients access implicit (body) memory of an early trauma, they will flood with emotion and become incapable of giv-ing any verbal feedback to the therapist. Lifespan Integration therapy can be used to resolve the early trauma and to integrate the dissoci-ated feeling states associated with the trauma, even without explicit memory of what happened. However, for this work to be successful without re-traumatizing the client, the LI therapist must be capable of staying profoundly attuned to her client. Before attempting this deli-cate work, therapists should have gained experience using LI with less traumatized clients, and should have taken the advanced (levels 2 and 3) Lifespan Integration training.

Lifespan Integration with Teenagers and Children

Young adults and teens are especially responsive to LI because:

1) Their neural systems are more plastic than those of adults,
2) They have not yet built up as many layers of defenses as adults have, and
3) Teens enjoy the active imagination and prefer the idea that they themselves are helping their own internal chil-dren, rather than needing to be helped by the therapist.

When working with teens or younger children, the memory cues should be expanded to include more memories within each year. This allows the child to see the passage of time without making too big a leap between memory cues. Use three or four chronological cues per year.

When working with young children, age seven and under, include the actual parent or caretaker in the session. The parent's presence allows the child to feel safe and to be more emotionally open to the work. The parent also helps the child to make the list of memory cues.

Lifespan Integration therapy can be used to help adolescents heal from the effects of divorce, trauma, or other early loss. Part of the emotional and psychological damage which children experience as a result of early loss is caused by the interpretation of the event which the child makes at the time of the loss. Lifespan Integration can be used to help a twelve-years-old child connect to his lonely, frightened four-years-old self. With coaching from the therapist, the twelve-years-old client can explain to the four-years-old self that the divorce or death or past trauma was not his fault, and that he is important and lovable. Going through the Time Line of images then connects the traumatized and alone four-years-old child self to the current self of the twelve-years-old. The coached internal conversation with the four-years-old combined with the integration through the LI Time Line will allow the twelve-years-old to let go of the earlier interpretation, and likewise to let go of fears and/or defenses that are no longer relevant to his current situation.

Using Lifespan Integration with Adopted Children

Children who are adopted often have an unknown history. These children may have attachment disorders or other psychological or behavioral problems which are related to their early experiences. Most adopted children, no matter how ideal the circumstances of the adoption, will later in life have questions and feelings about having been abandoned by their biological parents. Lifespan Integration can often be successfully used to resolve known or unknown early trauma and deficits in early attachment.

Work with the adoptive parents and the adopted child to create a memory cue list. The cues should incorporate as much factual information as is available about the child's birth and early life, including when and how the child came to live with the adopted parents. Use two or three memory cues for each year. Include the child's earliest memory (the first memory which she actually remembers) and continue with two or three memories per year all the way into present time.

Tell the child that her baby self needs to understand what happened and how she has grown up. Tell the child that you need her help to show her baby self how she grew up. Tell the child the way to do this is to see pictures in her mind about growing up, and the baby self will see them too. Then ask the child to imagine herself being born, and then to imagine self at each of the early stages of development. Add known events from the child's history when possible. For example, if the child was put in foster care at 8 months of age, add this to the cue for the crawling stage. Read all the cues, staying attuned to the child. Repeat the above two or more times. Depending on the age of the child, the adoptive parent sometimes holds the child during the session while the child 'shows' the story of her life to her baby self.

Working with Older Adults

When using Lifespan Integration therapy with older adults it is important to schedule plenty of time. A ninety minute session will generally be sufficient time to clear one trauma memory providing talking is kept to a minimum. Older adults have more years and more memories to sort through. Because older minds are in general less plastic than younger minds, older clients often seem to require more repetitions of the protocol to clear the source memory. With older clients, when clearing past trauma, it is not necessary to read a memory cue for every year. When clearing trauma with LI, it is more important to get through enough repetitions of the protocol than it is to touch on every year of the client's life. The therapist should read one cue for each year through age twenty or thirty. After that it is fine to read one cue for every two years, or even one for every three years. When skipping years, use odd years and then even years, or alternate going by two year intervals with three year intervals. When skipping years, do not leave out any important events, even if this means reading more cues. When working with an older client to build structure, as opposed to clearing trauma, you will need enough time for three repetitions of the Attunement protocol. When building structure, it is best to read a cue for every year. Ninety minutes is usually adequate for three repetitions of the Attunement protocol, providing talking is kept to a minimum.

Chapter Twelve
Common Obstacles to LI Processing

Client is Not Retrieving Memory Images Correctly

The client's repeated 'viewings' of chronologically laid out images of his life are key to neural integration. The goal of Lifespan Integration is to encourage neural networks to make new connections to one another which eventually create a more fluid map of self across space and time. In order for this process to become fluid, it is necessary for the client to allow the memories to surface spontaneously. One's ability to see oneself fluidly across time and space, or auto-noetic consciousness, is highly correlated with secure attachment and with neural integration.

There is not one correct way to 'see' each memory image. Each memory cue should bring the client back in time to a specific memory scene. Clients who are present in their bodies will also have good access to their right brain hemisphere. These clients will 'see' and feel an expansion of memories each time a specific cue is repeated. The expansion will be somehow related to the specific cue. Either more details about the memory cue will be remembered, or the client will be reminded of another event which is in some way related. Random jumping about with new unrelated memories entering in does not indicate integration. Neural integration is working at its best when clients are able to 'see' and feel the memory scene through all their senses. Clients who are well connected to their bodies will experience the memory of smells, sounds, and bodily and tactile sensations from the time of the memory cue. The best cues will point the client toward memories which are rich in sensory detail.

Generally just 'seeing' an image is not enough. Clients who are very dissociative can be good at bringing up the memory images, but usually they will not get much expansion from repetition to repetition. Expansion of memories should be effortless. Most clients with good memory recall are able to relax and allow images, smells, emotions, and insights to spontaneously enter consciousness.

Check with the client to make certain that the client has a sense of remembering, or of being 'in' the memory. In other words, differentiate between the internal 'viewing' of an actual memory scene,

95

versus the client's viewing a photographic image in his mind, but with no actual recall of ever having been there. If clients are retrieving images spontaneously, the images will become richer and more varied on each repetition of the protocol. More details will be remembered, and the memories will become more positive overall during each subsequent repetition.

When working with dissociative clients and clients with memory gaps, the therapist should read, for each year, the cue for that year which has the most potential to expand in a sensory direction. To encourage neural expansion, the therapist should continue to read the same memory cues on each subsequent repetition.

If the client has good memory recall and still is not getting images spontaneously, he is probably using a left brain process to 'remember' life events he has memorized such as which teacher he had for each grade in school, where he worked, etc. Some clients will make an effort to screen or censor the memory images as they surface. They may report that they didn't want to show the bad scenes to their child self, or that the memories seemed too mundane and they instead were looking for memories of important occasions. If the client is censoring his images, he is using a left brain process and integration will be minimal. Explain to the client that he will get better results from the therapy if he can allow the memories to come forward whether good, bad, or neutral.

When a client interrupts his process to tell you about the images or memories which are emerging, the process is not fluid, and less integration will occur. In addition there is the risk that by discussing other memory scenes, the client will activate the emotional networks associated with these memories. The therapist should continue with reading the memory cues, and explain to the client that the process works much better without interruptions. At the break the therapist can make a brief note of what came up for the client, but should make an effort to minimize discussion until after the client has gone through sufficient repetitions of the protocol.

Client Interrupts Process with Too Much Talking

During a Lifespan Integration session, the material that comes up for clients is often quite interesting. It is easy for both client and therapist to get distracted by the new memories and insights. Keep in mind that excessive talking derails the Lifespan Integration process for the following reasons:

- Talking takes the client into cognitions and language (left brain hemisphere) and away from the feelings and images (right brain) which need to be present for neural integration to occur.

- Talking breaks the flow of images by stopping to discuss one image.

- Talking uses up time, making it harder to complete the needed number of repetitions within the allotted time.

- Talking about a new memory, depending on the nature of the memory, has the potential to activate other neural networks and associated emotional and somatic memories.

There can be several reasons why clients interrupt their process with talking. Very often clients are preconditioned to think that talking is what therapy is all about. They have a hard time understanding why the therapist wouldn't need to know all the details of what comes up for them during a Lifespan Integration session. Some clients will use talking as a way to distance themselves from uncomfortable feelings. Others, who are not yet able to relax and trust the process, will use conversation as a way to take charge of the session. It is the job of the therapist to discourage any unnecessary conversation.

Clients who have become familiar with the Lifespan Integration protocol, and who have benefited from it are generally very good about keeping conversation to a minimum and offering up only the necessary feedback. The therapist should ask the client at the beginning of each session whether he wants to use his therapy session for talking or for LI therapy. Clients who have experienced the benefits of Lifespan Integration therapy often choose to do LI. Clients who choose to do LI are usually comfortable with the restrictions on talking.

Therapist Interrupts Process with Too Much Talking

For most analytically trained therapists the hardest part of learning to use Lifespan Integration is learning to trust the process. This requires that therapists disregard a lot of what they have learned previously. Even if the therapist is able to correctly analyze the client's problem, the analysis becomes irrelevant when using Lifespan Integration as a treatment modality.

If either the therapist or the client spends too much time talking, there may not be enough time for sufficient repetitions of the LI Time Line. Repetitions of the Time Line are where neural integration occurs and where the majority of the healing takes place. If the therapist talks too much when coaching the internal conversations, the child ego state will tune out both the therapist and the adult self. During the internal conversations, the child ego state will benefit more from brief statements which convey needed information. The time saved can be used for coached imaginal play between the adult client and his child self, or for additional repetitions of the Time Line of memories and images.

The Adult Self Has Trouble Entering the Memory Scene

When using LI to clear a past traumatic event, some clients have trouble imagining their adult selves entering the memory scene in Step 3. When this occurs it is usually because the adult client has become too identified with the child ego state in the memory scene, and has become disconnected from her adult strengths and capabilities. In other words, there is no adult self available to be brought into the scene. If in Step 3 the adult client reports having trouble entering the memory scene, begin reading the memory cues from the age of the targeted memory all the way to present time. This will reconnect the client with her current adult self. It may be necessary to go through the cues twice.

In some cases the adult self is fully present but feels overwhelmed at the prospect of going into the childhood trauma scene alone. Whenever indicated, invite the client to use any imaginal resources that would be helpful to her. Clients sometimes imagine bringing in police officers, social workers, or caretakers for younger siblings. Clients also sometimes choose to imaginally bring in friends or partners to help them, or spiritual guides, angels, or other religious figures.

Interference from Split off Parts of Self

When a normally cooperative client seems to be making a considerable effort to distract and disrupt a Lifespan Integration session, there is a good chance that the client's core Self has been temporarily overtaken by a Part of self who is feeling threatened about the prospect of integration. Often when an addicted Part of a client 'realizes' that it is becoming increasingly more difficult to hijack control of the client's self-system, this Part begins to interfere with the Lifespan Integration process. Parts of the self can only come into play when the weak executive function of the self-system is 'off-line.'

Clients with split-off parts which are powerful enough to periodically hijack the self-system will benefit most from sessions of the LI structure building protocols. With more and more presence of Self, dissociative states lose their ability to take over the self-system.

Client Dissociates during Step 6, the LI Time Line

Dissociative clients have a tendency to drift away into their thoughts when being led through their memory cues. Neural integration occurs when clients are present in their bodies as they remember (view and feel) the memory images. Dissociative clients are often accustomed to living in their thoughts, or in a fantasy world, disconnected from bodily sensations. Lifespan Integration therapy will increase their connection to body and emotion, and as this occurs they will unconsciously do things to defend against the unpleasant and unfamiliar sensations.

Dissociation can be countered to some degree by the following:

1) The therapist maintains an energetic connection to the client and stays attuned to the client throughout the Time Line. If the therapist finds self fighting an urge to fall asleep, it is likely that the client is dissociated.

2) The client must signal the therapist when she 'sees' each cued memory. When she doesn't signal, the therapist checks with her, asking: "Did you get that image?"

3) If the client seems to drift off when her eyes are closed, have her continue the process with her eyes open or half way open.

4) Dissociative clients should hold something with a strong aroma and should periodically smell it.

5) Watch the client's breathing. If needed, remind the client to breathe deeply.

Therapist Needs Lifespan Integration Therapy

The therapist's ability to stay present and grounded is a critical element of Lifespan Integration therapy. The therapist's calm presence transmits to the child ego state the energy the child needs to feel safe and contained. When using the LI Attunement protocol, the therapist's energetic connection with the client and with the client's baby self is similar to the ideal energetic resonance and attunement between parent and child during early development and attachment.

Therapists who are coherent, congruent, and integrated will be capable of staying present with their clients no matter what comes up in the processing. Therapists who have done their own healing work will get the best results when using Lifespan Integration with their clients. A therapist who is internally chaotic will not be able to transmit to the client and to the client's child or infant self the calm, loving, coherent state needed for optimal neural integration.

Client Is Undiagnosed D.I.D.

Some D.I.D. clients are not aware that they are D.I.D., and others are very good at covering their switching between alters or ego states. It is very possible for a therapist to be working with a D.I.D. client without realizing she is D.I.D. Lifespan Integration therapy is very useful for working with D.I.D. clients, but only if the client is able to keep her core self forward in her self system throughout the Lifespan Integration protocol. If the therapist is working with a D.I.D. client without awareness of the client's D.I.D. diagnosis, it is possible that switching between ego states during Step 6 is preventing integration from occurring. Often dissociative clients' bodies will jerk or spasm slightly with state shifts. If progress is not being made with Lifespan Integration therapy and there is a likelihood that the client could be undiagnosed D.I.D., try the modified Lifespan Integration protocol for working with D.I.D. clients.

Use of Marijuana and Other Medications

The active ingredients in marijuana block neural integration. Some therapists have had success using Lifespan Integration to help clients reduce intake of marijuana, and to eventually quit marijuana use/ abuse. If the client is able to refrain from smoking marijuana for even three days, the LI Attunement protocol can then be utilized to help her find better ways to self-soothe.

Benzodiazepines severely block the neural action needed for integration. Unfortunately benzos are frequently prescribed for anxiety disorders. Other medications such as opioids and other pain killers dampen neural action and seem to slow down progress with LI, but they do not entirely block integration. Selective Serotonin Reuptake Inhibitors (SSRI's) do not interfere significantly with Lifespan Integration except when the dose is so high that the client is too removed from her body. More data needs to be collected regarding which drugs and medications interfere with Lifespan Integration therapy.

Chapter Thirteen
Frequently Asked Questions

How much time is required for a Lifespan Integration session?

The recommended time for LI sessions depends on the age of the client and the experience of the therapist. For clients forty years old or older, a 75 to 80 minute session is preferable. With older clients, more repetitions of Steps 3–7 are usually required to clear the source memory. In addition, no matter what protocol is being used, older clients tend to need more repetitions, and with older clients each repetition takes longer simply because there are many more years to go through.

When first beginning to use Lifespan Integration therapy it is best to allow 75 to 80 minutes for each session. After the therapist has become familiar with the protocol, 50 minutes should be sufficient for most clients under forty years of age. Allow more time for dissociative clients.

Is it OK to deviate from the protocols as written in the book?

The protocols are meant to be guides. Therapists who understand the principals at work in Lifespan Integration will be able to vary the protocols to meet the individual needs of each client. The statements written in the book are general and sometimes will not apply. When using standard protocol LI to clear a trauma, often a child self will need attention more than information. Therapists who understand children's needs at various stages will be able to coach the adult client to give the child the information he needs, or to enter into an age appropriate interactive imagined experience with the child self.

Why does the therapist need to tell the adult client what to say and what to do with her child self?

When the adult client is regressed to being her child self in the past memory scene, feeling her emotions from that past event, she will not know, at that moment, what her child self needs to hear. This is true even if the adult client is a skilled child psychotherapist.

In order to think about what her child self needs, it would be necessary for the adult client to leave the child state and enter a more cognitive, adult state. To clear a past trauma, the client must remain 'hooked up' to the neural networks of the trauma memory. The adult client will be able to keep this connection intact only if she avoids cognition as much as possible.

What if the child self won't cooperate?

Clients with fragmented self systems will benefit most from the LI structure building protocols. If the decision is made to use standard protocol LI to clear trauma, the therapist should explain to the client beforehand that trauma clearing work means sitting through how-ever many repetitions are needed to clear the trauma. If the client agrees to this, and yet half way through the session says she doesn't want to watch the scenes from her life any more, most likely the child self has taken over the executive function.

In these cases, simply instruct the adult client to inform the child self that she doesn't have to watch the images. She can read a book or cover her eyes while the therapist continues to read the cues for as many repetitions as are needed. If the client hears the memory cues, she will 'see' the memory images. All parts of the client's self system will see the images to some degree as there is only one mind and one visual cortex. This will be sufficient for completion of the trauma clearing session. To avoid this problem, when working with fragmented clients, use the Lifespan Integration Attunement proto-col and the other structure building protocols until there is a solid enough core self to proceed with clearing any memories of trauma.

What if clients have memory gaps?

The memory cue list doesn't have to have actual memories for every year of the client's life. Memory gaps of one or two years are acceptable. If the client has no memory at all for a certain age, simply ask the client to imagine herself at that age standing in the neighbor-hood where she lived then, or in front of a school she attended, or in the house she lived in.

Do not begin LI therapy with clients who have memory gaps of three years or more. Work first with these clients to construct a list of memory cues. Spend a few weeks with the client discussing her history and life. Work together in session to create a list of mem-ory cues. At first it is not critical for the memories be in the cor-rect sequence or even to be attached to the correct age. After the memory cue list has been completed, begin therapy with several sessions of LI structure building protocols. As more new memories enter into consciousness, the client may want to re-write the memory cues, adding new memories and rearranging the others in the correct chronological order.

Does the client need to see self in the memory scene?

No, it is not necessary for the client to see himself in the memory scene. Integration works best when clients can re-experience the memory. Most clients report a mixture of sensory input as they re-experience memories. Instead of 'seeing' the memory scene, some clients may remember what they felt or heard or smelled or tasted. Any sensory memory will contribute to integration. Some dissociative clients are quite good at 'seeing' without really feeling. Simply 'seeing' an image while dissociated from bodily sensations and emotions will not contribute to neural integration.

It is most common for the memories to come up as they were originally viewed, from the eyes of the child self. Sometimes the client will see only parts of the memory scene. It is not necessary to see the whole picture. Very likely more of the memory will surface on subsequent repetitions of the Time Line. It is important, however, for the client to have a sense of remembering the actual event. Clients may use photographs to trigger their memories, but it is necessary that they actually remember the photographed event for neural integration to be effective.

When reading the memory cues during Step 6 it works best to say: "Remember learning to ride your bike." In other words, say "remember" and then insert the cue, or simply read the cue. Saying: "See yourself riding your bike", causes many clients to move outside of themselves to see the image, rather than to experience the feeling of riding a bike.

What if the client feels physical pain during LI?

It is quite common for physical pain associated with a source memory to come into the client's body for release during Lifespan Integration. LI seems to access and integrate implicit and somatic memories. Occasionally the pain will increase with the first two or three repetitions of the protocol as the client connects more deeply to the memory. As the client continues with repetitions of Steps 3 through

7, her body-mind will fully understand that the event was long ago. When the body-mind understands this, any parts of the memory which are no longer adaptive for the self system are released. This includes the neurological and somatic memory of the physical pain.

Can LI therapy be used to treat addictions?

Yes, the LI Attunement and LI trauma clearing protocols can be used to help treat addictions. The LI therapy will be more likely to succeed if the addicted client participates concurrently in a program or treatment group specific to his addiction. The Lifespan Integration Attunement protocol focused on affect regulation can be very helpful for recovering addicts who are committed to their sobriety. Most people with addictions experienced trauma, neglect, or both during early childhood. They often have trouble with intimate relationships and with affect regulation. They often use their addictions and/ or compulsive behaviors in an attempt to regulate their emotional states. Regular sessions of the Lifespan Integration Attunement protocol, spaced weekly or every two weeks, with an experienced and coherent LI therapist will 'teach' addicted clients' body-mind systems better ways to self-soothe and to regulate emotion.

People with addictions do not have strong core selves. The weak core self is easily pushed aside when the addicted part chooses to use the addictive substance, or to participate in the addictive behavior. Repeated sessions of the Lifespan Integration Attunement protocol will strengthen the core self of the addicted client. Addicted parts of self often feel increasingly threatened as the integration which occurs with LI brings about a more coherent self system. As the core Self becomes stronger, there will likely be increased attempts by the client (coming from the addict within the client) to avoid or to sabotage the Lifespan Integration therapy sessions.

Note:

An incomplete session of Lifespan Integration therapy could potentially activate a client's early trauma history. Therapists working with addicts should have training and skills specific to addiction and recovery, and should use LI when the addictive client has attained a certain stable level of sobriety. When using LI with recovering addicts, the therapist will need to stay profoundly attuned to the client throughout the session. Activating trauma memory in a client without fully clearing it could possibly lead to relapse.

What if the adult client dislikes her child self?

Sometimes during the active imagination part of the Lifespan Integration protocol, when the adult client is instructed to enter the past scene to interact with the child, the adult will report that she doesn't like her child self. When the adult client reports that she dislikes her child self, it is likely that the 'adult' client is not representing the total Self, but rather is a part-self. If the adult client reports that she doesn't like her child self, switch to using the LI Attunement protocol. After many sessions of LI Attunement, the client's core self will be sufficiently strengthened, and the client will be able to feel affection and compassion for all her child selves.

What if the child self dislikes the adult self?

This is somewhat common and is not really a problem as long as the adult self likes the child self. Sometimes the child self is angry at the adult self and doesn't like her. Child ego states who are split off by the self system and are left in the past often feel hurt and abandoned. In Step 7 of the LI protocol, a very common question coming from a child ego state is: "Why did you leave me?" Another commonly asked question is: "Do you love me?"

When the child self doesn't like the adult, instruct the adult client to tell her child self how important the child is to her. Instruct the adult to apologize to the child for leaving her in the past trauma scene. Have the adult client tell her child self that she left her in the past because she had to grow up, but now that she has grown up she has come back to get the child and she will not leave her again. Instruct the adult client to attend to her child self's needs and to imaginally spend time with her child self. Coach age appropriate ways in which the adult client can reach out to her child self and nurture her both in the peaceful place and in the current home in Step 7. Coach a behavior and then allow 15-30 seconds of silence while the adult client imagines interacting with her child self, nurturing her and showing her that she is important to the adult. Usually by the third repetition of the protocol, the child self has begun to warm up to the adult.

What if the child self doesn't trust the adult?

The child self in the source memory may not trust any adults. The child has been frozen in time, and must rely on her limited experience of adults to determine whether or not adults are safe. If the client experienced mostly abuse and neglect from the adults in her early environment, her child self may not understand that some adults are safe and well-intentioned. It is sometimes effective to have the adult client explain to the younger child selves that adults can be safe, however this is often not sufficiently convincing.

If the child self doesn't trust the adult self of the client and doesn't want to come with her to a peaceful place, the therapist should instruct the adult client to tell her child self that she will prove to her that she has grown up and become part of the adult. The therapist then reads the memory cues, beginning with the first cue after the source memory and ending in present time. Reviewing her life in this way will begin to show the child self that she has grown and is now part of the adult. She will see along the Time Line that some adults are trustworthy. Usually after one journey through the LI Time Line, the child self will trust the adult enough to go with her to the peaceful place on the next repetition of the protocol.

What if the child self doesn't want to leave the past?

Occasionally a client will report that his child self in the source memory scene is unwilling to leave the past. Either the child state likes it there, or he is trying to resolve an issue that was a problem for him at that point in his history. Because he is frozen in time, the child self doesn't realize that the problem he is trying to resolve is no longer an issue. For example: A child may feel the need to stay in the past because he is worried if he leaves no one will be there to care for younger siblings.

When a child state is resistant to leaving the past, ask the adult client to explain to the child self that the past exists now only as a memory. The child self has grown up and become the adult client, and staying in the past is not really an option. Then lead the client through the Time Line of memory cues beginning with the cue directly after the source memory where the child self is stuck, and ending in the present. After reaching the last memory cue in present time, ask the client to imagine bringing his child self into the present to show him where he lives now. Repeat as many times as are needed to convince the child self that the past is truly past.

What if in Step 1 the client goes back to a positive memory?

Sometimes in Step 1 of the standard protocol, the client will begin with the current problem, follow her body-mind system, and will end up at a positive memory. When this occurs it is usually because the client's system needs to resource itself (by integrating a positive memory and other associated positive memories along the Time Line) before the client is ready to go to a more traumatic memory.

When the client goes back to a positive memory in Step 1, simply follow the protocol and have the adult self enter the past scene, engage with the child self, and show the child self the Time Line to integrate the positive memory and the other positive associated memories which will spontaneously come up along the Time Line of memories and images. After the positive memory has been integrated, providing enough time remains in the session, return to the presenting problem (Step 1) and again have the client focus on what she feels in her body. The client will probably now be ready to go back to the source memory most connected to the presenting problem.

Resourcing at the beginning of an LI session occurs infrequently. More commonly the resourcing during Lifespan Integration occurs spontaneously toward the end of the session when the client is going through the last repetitions of the Time Line. Each subsequent repetition of the Time Line brings up more positive, resourcing memories.

How does Lifespan Integration differ from other techniques?

Lifespan Integration therapy differs from other methods in that it utilizes repetitions of the client's life narrative, in visual and sensory form, to bring about integration and increased coherence within the client's self system. In has been known for some time that neural integration in young children occurs through the co-construction of the autobiographical narrative. Anecdotal evidence shows that neural integration in adults occurs during Lifespan Integration therapy through the same mechanism.

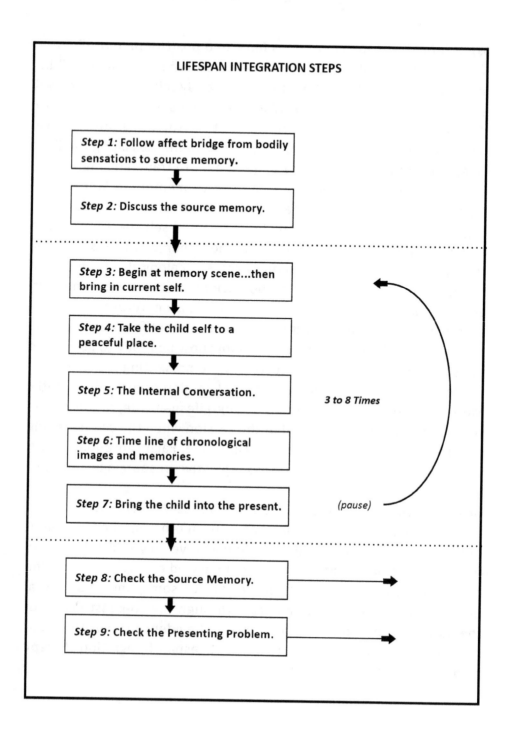

LIFESPAN INTEGRATION STEPS

Step 1: Follow affect bridge from bodily sensations to source memory.

Step 2: Discuss the source memory.

Step 3: Begin at memory scene...then bring in current self.

Step 4: Take the child self to a peaceful place.

Step 5: The Internal Conversation.

Step 6: Time line of chronological images and memories.

Step 7: Bring the child into the present.

3 to 8 Times

(pause)

Step 8: Check the Source Memory.

Step 9: Check the Presenting Problem.

Preparing a Memory Que List

Memory Cue Instructions for Clients

When first beginning to do Lifespan Integration therapy, many people are unable to get a spontaneous flow of memories during the Time Line step of the LI protocol. This is the step when the adult self proves to his or her inner child self that time has passed, and the child has grown up. Even people who have fluid memory recall for most years of their lives may have some gaps or stretches of years where memories are much harder to access. The memory cue list will allow you to recall visual and other sensory aspects of each memory from the right brain hemisphere; and this will improve your ability to recall more of your life. The goal for integration is to move you toward a more free association of memories as you go from year to year visually. You will notice as you experience a Lifespan Integration session, that when a memory cue is read to you, other memories from that same time frame will spontaneously begin to enter your mind.

To prepare the memory cue list, begin with your earliest memory. For most people the earliest memory will be of age 2 or 3. Try to remember at least one memory for each year of your life. For each cue, write down the calendar year, the age you were at the time of the memory, and a word or phrase that will remind you of the memory when your therapist reads the word or phrase to you. Your therapist doesn't have to understand what the cues stand for, however it is important for the therapist to be aware of any cues which will remind you of traumatic events. You will need only one cue for each year; however for variation it is helpful to have 2 or 3 cues for each year. Be sure to separate your cues with a / mark. Your therapist will read only one cue per year, but she may alternate cues used on different repetitions. The dates and ages will help you to organize the cues chronologically, but during the LI session your therapist will read only the cues.

Try to think of one memory for each year of your life, from your earliest memory all the way to the present. Cues which can evoke the memory of smells, tastes, sounds, and tactile sensations work best to promote integration. For example the cue: "learning to swim" could bring back the smell of the water or chlorine, the feel of the water, the sounds of splashing, etc. Memories used for cues should be specific to one year only. For example, "working at Microsoft" would be a confusing memory cue for someone who worked there for several years. In this case the cue would need to be more specific, as: "fender bender in Microsoft parking lot". Record your memory cues chronologically. Write legibly or type your memory cues on your computer. The cues should be events that you actually remember as opposed to a scene which you have seen in a photograph but when you look at the photo you don't recall having been in the scene. The cues can also be the name of a friend you spent time with at a certain age, or a place from the past which you remember.

The memories do not need to be significant in any way. Even remembering what a house or school building looked like is enough detail if that is all you remember. Be sure to include significant events which impacted your life such as deaths of people important to you, other traumatic events which affected you, marriages, divorces, births, etc. The memory cues should cover your entire life, from your earliest memory all the way to the present year.

Sample cues for ages 10 – 13.
1989 Age 10 – best friend Gus
1990 Age 11 – moved to Chicago / started middle school
1991 Age 12 – summer camp with Will
1992 Age 13 – skiing with Jen / 8th grade graduation

These memory cue instructions may be copied and given to clients.

Glossary

Autonoetic Consciousness—self-knowing, the ability to see the self across time

Ego State—A type of self-state which is associated with the ego or works through the ego. An ego state can also be seen as a neural network. (See 'self state' below.)

Explicit Memory—memory which develops in the second year of life. Requires focal attention for encoding. Involves recollection of self in time.

Implicit Memory—sensory memory (bodily, behavioral, perceptual, and emotional) is present at birth, does not require focal attention for encoding, no memory of self in time, no sense of recollecting.

Integration—The organization of various traits, feelings, attitudes, etc. into one harmonious personality. (from Webster's New World Dictionary)

Neural Network—A network of neurons linked by synaptic connections. The human brain contains billions of neurons, and millions of networks of neurons. These networks are interconnected to varying degrees through the integrating processes of the brain.

Neural Plasticity—The condition of neural plasticity exists when many neurons are firing at the same time, increasing the likelihood that new synaptic firing patterns will occur. New learning and changes in old patterns are more likely to occur under conditions of neural plasticity.

Part—A self-state or ego state with a life of its own, existing outside of ego control.

Self-state—a state of the self. A particular pattern of neurons firing together which create a certain body sensation, emotion, mood, etc. which are particular to that specific neural network. Infants and young children exist as a series of self-states which are later integrated to form a cohesive self system.

References

Almaas, A.H. *The Point of Existence: Transformations of narcissism in self-realization,* Boston, MA: Shambhala Publications, 2000.

Almaas, A.H. *Essence,* Boston, MA: Red Wheel/Weiser, LLC, 1998.

Almaas, A.H. *The Pearl Beyond Price, Integration of personality into being: An object relations approach,* Boston, MA: Shambhala Publications, 1988.

Almaas, A.H. *Elements of the Real in Man,* Boston, MA: Shambhala Publications, 1987.

Almaas, A.H. *The Freedom to Be,* Boston, MA: Shambhala Publications, 1989.

Almaas, A.H. B*eing and the Meaning of Life,* Berkeley, CA: Diamond Books, 1990.

Almaas, *A.H. Indestructible Innocence,* Boston, MA: Shambhala Publications, 1987.

Almaas, A.H. *The Void: Inner spaciousness and ego structure,* Boston, MA: Shambhala Publications, 1986.

Casteneda, Carlos. *The Active Side of Infinity,* New York, N.Y.: Harper-Collins Publishers, Inc, 1998.

Chopra, Deepak. *Quantum Healing: Exploring the frontiers of mind/body medicine,* New York, N.Y.: Bantam Books, 1989.

Cozolino, Louis. 2002. *The neuroscience of psychotherapy: Building and rebuilding the human brain.* New York, NY: W.W. Norton and Co.

Damasio, Antonio R. 1994. *Descartes' error: Emotion, reason, and the human brain.* New York, NY: Grosset / Putnam

Goswami, Amit. *The Self-Aware Universe: How consciousness creates the material world*, New York, N.Y.: Penguin Putnam Inc, 1993.

Hannah, Barbara. 1981. *Encounters with the soul: Active imagination as developed by C.G. Jung*. Santa Monica, CA: Sigo Press.

Johnson, Robert A. 1986. *Inner work: Using dreams & active imagination for personal growth*. New York, NY: HarperCollins Publishers

LeDoux, Joseph. 1996. *The emotional brain: The mysterious underpinnings of emotional life*. New York, NY: Simon and Schuster.

LeDoux, Joseph. 2002. *Synaptic self: How our brains become who we are*. New York, NY: Penguin Putnam.

Levine, Peter A. 1997. *Waking the tiger, Healing trauma: The innate capacity to transform overwhelming experiences*. Berkeley, CA: North Atlantic Books.

Mindell, Arnold. *Quantum Mind: The edge between physics and psychology*, Portland, OR: Lao Tse Press, 2000.

Nadeau, Robert & Kafatos, Menas. *The Non-Local Universe: The new physics and matters of the mind*, New York, N.Y.: Oxford University Press, Inc, 1999.

Nhat Hanh, Thich. *The Miracle of Mindfulness*, Boston, MA: Beacon Press, 1975.

Schore, A.N. 1994. *Affect regulation and the origin of the self: The neurobiology of emotional development*. Hillsdale, NJ: Lawrence Erlbaum Associates.

Schore, Allan N. 2003. *Affect dysregulation and disorders of the self*. New York, NY: W.W. Norton and Company, Inc.

Schwartz, Jeffrey M. & Begley, Sharon. 2002. *The mind and the brain: Neuroplasticity and the power of mental force.* New York, NY: Harper Collins Publishers, Inc.

Schwartz, Richard C. 1995. *Internal family systems therapy.* New York, NY: The Guilford Press.

Siegel, Daniel J. 1999. *The developing mind: Toward a neurobiology of interpersonal experience.* New York, NY: The Guilford Press.

Siegel, Daniel J. 2012. The developing mind: How relationships and the Brain interact to shape who we are, New York, NY: The Guilford Press.

Rinpoche, Sogyal. *The Tibetan Book of Living and Dying,* New York, N.Y.: HarperCollins Publishers, Inc, 1992.

Talbot, Michael. *The Holographic Universe,* New York, N.Y.: Harper-Collins Publishers, Inc, 1991.

Watkins, J.G., *The Affect Bridge: A hypnoanalytic technique, International Journal of Clinical and Experimental Hypnosis,* 19, pp. 21-27, 1971.

Disclaimer

This book provides information about Lifespan Integration, a revolutionary new therapeutic method which helps clients to change on a deep body-mind level. When administered by trained and experienced psychotherapists, Lifespan Integration therapy allows survivors of childhood neglect and abuse to build new neural structures, and to let go of patterns which no longer serve them. Neuroscience shows us that due to the way in which neural networks operate in the body-mind, current structures ('operating systems') must break down before new neural networks can be built or re-structured. Reading this book will not give therapists the skills they need to begin practicing Lifespan Integration therapy. A therapist who attempts this method without proper training runs the risk of dys-regulating a fragile client's self-system.

The efficacy of Lifespan Integration therapy is well supported by anecdotal evidence; however formal research has not yet been conducted. As such, Peggy Pace and Lifespan Integration, LLC do not guarantee nor do they make any express or implied warranties with regard to expected patient responses or the efficacy of Lifespan Integration therapy. Lifespan Integration, LLC recommends that all professionals who use LI therapy fully disclose to their clients that Lifespan Integration is a new therapy, and has not yet been fully researched.

Best outcomes with Lifespan Integration therapy result when the administering therapist is internally coherent, and is able to remain energetically and emotionally present throughout the LI session. Psychotherapists who have done their own body-mind healing work will be better able to stay present with the client to contain any emotional material which may emerge during LI processing. Therapists, psychologists, and psychiatrists who wish to use this new method are advised to attend a Lifespan Integration training workshop. At a training workshop, mental health practitioners observe Lifespan Integration sessions live and on DVD, and practice and experience Lifespan Integration under supervision.

For dates and locations of future trainings:
https://lifespanintegration.com

Biographical Information

Peggy Pace is a licensed mental health counselor and marriage and family therapist in Washington State. Peggy Pace received a Bachelor of Science degree in Chemistry from the University of Washington in 1969, and a Master of Arts degree in Counseling Psychology from Antioch University in 1985. For the past thirty years, Pace has specialized in working with adults who were traumatized as children.

In 2002, Peggy Pace developed the Lifespan Integration technique while working with clients in her private practice. In 2003 she self-published the first edition of her book, *Lifespan Integration: Connecting Ego States through Time*. Since 2004 Pace has been dividing her time between her private practice in Washington State, and traveling and teaching Lifespan Integration throughout the United States and Europe.

CPSIA information can be obtained
at www.ICGtesting.com
Printed in the USA
FFHW012146081119
56000741-61877FF